INTERPRETING RELIG

General editors: Judith Everington and

C000090319

Christians

GEOFF ROBSON

Heinemann

Heinemann Educational Publishers
Halley Court, Jordan Hill, Oxford OX2 8EJ
MADRID ATHENS PARIS FLORENCE PRAGUE WARSAW PORTSMOUTH NH
CHICAGO SAO PAULO SINGAPORE TOKYO MELBOURNE AUCKLAND
IBADAN GABORONE JOHANNESBURG

First published 1995

99 98 97 96 95

10 9 8 7 6 5 4 3 2 1

British Library Cataloguing in Publication Data
A catalogue record for this book is available from the British Library

ISBN 0 435 39091 0

Designed and typeset by Artistix, Oxon
Produced by Mandarin Offset
Printed and bound in Hong Kong

Acknowledgements

The author would like to thank the young people featured in this book, their families and the Christian communities to which they belong, for their willing help and co-operation.
The Warwick RE Project would like to thank: Eleanor Nesbitt of the Warwick Religions and Education Research Unit who conducted the initial fieldwork on which this book is based; the St Gabriel's Trust and the Dulverton Trust for financial support.

The publishers would like to thank the following for permission to reproduce copyright material.
The estate of Mel Calman for the cartoon on p. 39; Christian Aid for the extract from 'Why Christian Aid?' on p. 39 and for the Christian Aid Week poster on p. 52, reproduced by permission of © Christian Aid, PO Box 100, London, SE1 7RT; Church of England Board for Social Responsibility for the extract from *Peacemaking in a Nuclear Age* on p. 50; Coventry Christian Fellowship for the quotations on pp. 52 and 60; the Department of Religious Education, the Orthodox Church in America for the extract from *We Pray to God: A Prayer Book for Children*, © the Orthodox Church in America 1973, on p. 23; Nicholas Elias for the extract from *The Divine Liturgy Explained* on p. 26; the Farmington Institute for Christian Studies, Manchester College, Oxford for the extracts from *The Farmington Papers*, No. SC1, 'Science and Christianity 1: Taking Science Seriously' by Dr John Polkinghorne, reproduced by permission, on pp. 40 and 41; Steve Kelly for the song lyrics on p. 29, © Steve Kelly 1993, used by permission; Rose Ketterer for the quotation on p. 63; London Yearly Meeting of the Religious Society of Friends for the extracts from *Christian Faith and Practice in the Society of Friends*, © the Religious Society of Friends (Quakers) in Britain, 1960, on pp. 15, 30, 45, 46, 52 and 61, and for the extract from *Encounter with Silence* by John Punshon on p. 30, reproduced with permission; John Mohr for his song 'He Who Began a Good Work', © Birdwing Music Alliance Media Limited CopyCare, on p. 63; Oxford University Press and Cambridge University Press for the extracts from the *Revised English Bible*, © OUP and CUP 1989, on pp. 15, 22, 32, 33, 34, 40, 42, 44, 45, 51, 52 and 55; Scripture Union for the extracts from *One to One* and *A Church for all Ages*, reproduced by permission, on pp. 17, 18 and 25; Transworld Publishers for the extracts from *A Brief History of Time* by Stephen Hawking on pp. 40 and 41; Vallentine, Mitchell & Co Ltd for the extract from *The Diary of Anne Frank*, 1954, on p. 18; English translations of 'The Lord's Prayer' and 'Nicene Creed', on pp. 22, 40 and 42, by the International Consultation on English Texts.

The publishers would like to thank the following for permission to reproduce photographs.
AFF/AFS Amsterdam p. 19; Circa Photo Library pp. 11, 21, 55; City of Manchester Art Galleries p. 7 (below); Coventry Christian Fellowship pp. 36 (right), 46 (both); Eleanor Nesbitt pp. 35, 49; Format/Jacky Chapman p. 48; Format/Joanne O'Brien p. 58; Format/Maggie Murray p. 53; June Todd pp. 16, 32; Last Resort Picture Library p. 54; Misereor Medienproduktion und Vertriebsgesellschaft mbH, copyright © 1990, for Motif No. 1 'The Kingdom of God is like a leaven' from the Misereor Lenten Veil 'Biblical Women – Guides to the Kingdom of God' painted by Lucy D'Souza p. 22; Network/Mike Goldwater p. 47; Peter J Roberts pp. 10 (below), 27 (left), 45; Quaker Tapestry Scheme pp. 9, 31, 57; Rex Features/ Kevin Weaver p. 51; Roger Scruton pp. 15, 59; Ronald Sheridan/Ancient Art and Architecture Collection p. 23; Rosemary Jackson pp. 24 (both), 26, 27 (right), 28 (both), 33, 34, 63 (both); Tony Hallas/ Science Photo Library p. 40 (left); Will and Deni McIntyre/Science Photo Library p. 40 (right); Woodmansterne p. 61. All other photographs were supplied by the author.

Main cover photograph by the British Library. This photograph, which shows the decorated 'cross-carpet' page preceding St Luke's Gospel from the Lindisfarne Gospels (*circa* 698 CE), is also used for the background image throughout the book.

The publishers have made every effort to trace copyright holders. However, if any material has been incorrectly acknowledged, we would be pleased to correct this at the earliest opportunity.

Contents

Teachers' notes　　Judith Everington and Robert Jackson

The Warwick RE Project's *Interpreting Religions* series for Key Stage 3 offers teachers and students a newly developed approach to Religious Education and an opportunity to work with original material taken from studies of religious communities in Britain conducted at the University of Warwick. The method aims to develop students' skills in interpreting religious ways of life through engaging with a range of source materials. The materials also encourage students to relate what they have studied to their own questions and concerns.

Representing religions

The materials do not represent religions as rigid and unified belief systems. Instead, the Warwick RE Project (WREP) approach draws attention to the diversity that is to be found within religions and to the personal and social nature of religious life. It also recognizes that religions need to be viewed from different perspectives if a balanced picture is to be given.

Instead of thinking of a religion as a set of beliefs and values, each religion is pictured as a relationship between individuals, the religious (and sometimes ethnic) groups to which they belong, and the wider religious tradition. This model enables students to appreciate the diversity within a religion, but also allows the identification of some common concepts and values.

The individual is a person with a religious background whose views and experiences enable the student to relate to religious material in a personal context. Each book introduces four individual young people of about the same age as the target readership of the book.

The membership group may be a sect, movement, denomination, an ethnic or social group or a combination of these. The four young people introduced in each book belong to a variety of religious and ethnic groups within one religious tradition.

The tradition is the religion, in the broadest sense. All the individuals introduced and the religious groups that they belong to are part of the tradition. Students are encouraged to see how individuals and groups relate to the wider tradition. Sometimes features common to the tradition are introduced (such as the Bible in the case of the Christian tradition). Sometimes other parts of the tradition are introduced for comparison.

Interpreting religions

Any attempt to understand a religion necessarily involves making interpretations. This is true of the individuals and groups featured in the books, who offer various interpretations of the same religion. It also holds true for students who encounter the material in the books. Students will come from many different religious and non-religious backgrounds, but they will all have some experiences they can draw on in helping them to interpret ways of life that might be unfamiliar to them.

The two interpretive methods developed in the activities are:

- **examining the relationship between individuals, the groups they belong to and the wider religious tradition.** Sometimes there is an emphasis on the relationship between individuals and their religious membership groups; sometimes the group's place in the wider tradition will be examined, or some aspect of a group's religious life will be compared with that of another group within the same tradition
- **making connections between the students' ideas, emotions and experiences and those of people introduced in the books.** By moving to and fro between their own world and the world of the 'insider', comparing and contrasting ideas, feelings and attitudes, students are helped to develop their understanding of another way of life.

Edification

Engagement with another's way of life has the potential to make an impact upon the students' own thinking and attitudes. The WREP approach encourages students to do more than reconstruct the religious lives of others. It also encourages them to relate the material studied to issues which are of concern to themselves.

The activities

Each book is divided into discrete but related units which offer a range of source material and a sequence of activities designed to encourage the development of interpretive skills.

Making it clear activities are designed to ensure that students have familiarized themselves with some of the basic facts and ideas featured in the unit before proceeding to interpretive tasks.

Building bridges is the title given to activities which encourage students to draw on their own experiences or on familiar ideas in order to interpret material featured in the unit. The aim here is to encourage the student to focus upon personal knowledge and experience which can be related (by analogy) to material from the religious tradition. The familiar is used to make sense of – or to gain insights into – the unfamiliar.

Working it out activities are designed to encourage students to begin the process of interpretation by relating material drawn from one of the three levels – individual, membership group, tradition – to material drawn from another level. The aim here is to bring two pieces of material together so that each sheds light upon the other.

Thinking it through activities encourage students to use material from a religious tradition as a stimulus to reflecting upon matters of personal significance or concern. The aim here is to encourage students to examine or re-examine aspects of their own lives and thinking in the light of questions, issues or experiences which are encountered in particular religious traditions, but which also have universal significance.

1 Introduction

This book

This book is about four young Christians. It is about the different ways in which they live their lives, make choices and decisions and try to make sense of their own experiences and the world around them. In doing these things, each young person is influenced by the particular Christian group to which he or she belongs and by the beliefs, values and writings (the tradition) which are shared by most Christians. But each young person is *unique* and each of them can have an influence upon their own Christian group and upon the whole Christian tradition.

Whether you are from a religious background or not, this book is also about you and your own ideas, opinions and experiences. It is about the things that influence you and the ways in which you have an influence upon others and upon the world around you.

Using this book

Working with this book, you will find some things familiar (perhaps because you are a Christian yourself), but you will also discover things which are new and unfamiliar. Some of these things will be about individual people, some will be about the different groups that they belong to, and some will be about things which are shared in common by different individuals and groups.

Your task will be to try to make sense of or *interpret* what you find by taking part in a series of activities. These will ask you to:

- sort out some information about the Christian tradition and about what being a Christian means to different people (**Making it clear**)
- use your own ideas and experiences to help you understand what it might be like to live, act or believe as a Christian (**Building bridges**)
- get a better picture of what an idea or experience might mean by looking at what different Christian people have to say about it (**Working it out**)
- use the ideas and experiences described in this book as a starting point for thinking about your own ideas, opinions and experiences (**Thinking it through**).

The young people

The four young people who appear in this book belong to four different Christian groups or denominations – the Church of England, the Religious Society of Friends, the Greek Orthodox Church and the Coventry Christian Fellowship. Each young person was interviewed and extracts from these interviews are included throughout this book. Units 2–5 introduce you to each young person and to the Christian denomination to which they belong.

Andrew

Alice

Stacey

Abigail

2 *Andrew and the Church of England*

Andrew

About Andrew

Andrew found out his name means 'strong' and thinks
  his parents chose it after one of Jesus' disciples.
Has no brothers or sisters.
Father is a research chemist in a large textile firm.
Mother is a doctor in general practice in a mining town.
One family pet, a rabbit.
Keen on model railways.
Chief interests: music and magic!
Plays the violin in a youth orchestra and is learning to be a conjurer.
Practising and performing take up most of his time.
Goes to a youth group at his church one night a week.
Family activities include walking (usually on Saturday afternoons) and going to worship
  on Sundays to Christ Church, their local parish church, one of many within the larger
  denomination called the Church of England or the Anglican Church.

About the Church of England

The Church of England has a history going back to the sixth century CE when Christian missionaries (see page 13) were sent to England by the bishop of Rome (or Pope). Others came from Scotland.

It is organized in large districts called dioceses, each under the authority of a bishop. Dioceses are grouped together in two larger units called provinces.
Each has an archbishop, the senior one at Canterbury, the other at York.

Dioceses are subdivided into smaller units called parishes, each under the care of a parish priest or vicar. Some parishes are a section of a town, others the size of a village. The ideal is to have a church established in every place for all who live there.

The Church of England has changed, particularly during the Reformation at the time of the Tudors and Stuarts when:

- Henry VIII separated it from the authority of Rome
- a *Book of Common Prayer* and an English translation of the Bible (the *King James* or *Authorized Version*) replaced Latin as the language of public worship
- priests and bishops were allowed to marry.

And more recently when:

- British Christians took the Anglican (Church of England) form of Christianity to other parts of the world
- the Queen and Parliament no longer had direct rule over the Church in England
- it got its own 'parliament', the General Synod, which can make decisions
- in 1994 it decided that women could become priests in the Church of England.

A Christ Church, Cheylesmore, Coventry

The Anglican Church feels that it is part of national and local society. Andrew's parish is just one of 160 in the diocese of Coventry.

'Christ Church had one of the three great church spires of Coventry, together with the Cathedral and Holy Trinity. We were bombed out of the town centre and moved to this building some 35 years ago.'
(Vicar of Christ Church, Cheylesmore)

B John Piper's painting of Coventry Cathedral after it was bombed in 1940

3 Alice and the Religious Society of Friends

About Alice

Alice was born in the house which is still her home.

Has one older brother, Matthew.

Father is an engineer in the electricity industry.

Mother is a computer programmer in a car factory.

Is keen on horse riding, when she can borrow a friend's pony.

Enjoys music, plays the viola.

Plays hockey, in goal, for a school team.

Has most fun helping backstage in drama productions.

'When you're flipping switches around everyone thinks you're dead professional and you really know what you're doing!'

Belongs to two youth organizations, one meets during the week in a school hall, the other on Sundays at the place of worship her family attend. This is the Hill Street Meeting House of the Religious Society of Friends, usually called 'Quakers' (a name that was given them by people opposed to their ideas).

Alice

About the Society of Friends

The Society of Friends began in the seventeenth century when George Fox had particular experiences of God. These led him to teach a different sort of Christianity from the other Churches. The Society is different in several ways.

'When we gather for worship we gather in silence, usually in a fairly plain place. There only needs to be a room for people to sit in. We don't have a set of teachings people have to learn and accept. But we do believe that each individual person has "that of God" within them.

George Fox felt that he'd been given a message that you didn't need a "mediator" to link you with God. So we don't have priests, ministers, people paid to lead.'

(Alice's mother)

The Society of Friends is organized in a series of regular meetings linked together locally and nationally. The 'London Yearly Meeting' consists of members of 'Monthly Meetings'. These cover an area roughly equivalent to a county. Within them local 'Meetings' are responsible for the individual meeting houses and their activities.

There are Quakers in many parts of the world, particularly the USA where some of the first Quakers settled.

A Hill Street Friends Meeting House, Coventry

In the past the Society was persecuted because Quakers refused to fight in wars and to swear formal 'oaths' in law courts. Their practice of only calling people 'Friend' was considered disrespectful by those used to special titles, like lords and magistrates.

The Society of Friends has contributed to industry and commerce through firms founded by Quakers such as Cadbury and Rowntree in confectionery and Lloyds and Barclay's banks. It has also contributed to the relief of suffering in prisons and in ambulance units in both world wars.

Making it clear

The word 'meeting' seems to have more than one meaning for Quakers including:
- a place to meet for worship
- the actual act of worship
- the people who meet locally to worship
- the way the society is organized, regionally and nationally.

Why do you think Quakers use the word 'meeting' rather than 'church'?

Write down your ideas and compare them with a partner.

Building bridges

Write down some of the things that you feel strongly about, for example pollution, racism, animal rights. Give your reasons to a partner.

Working it out

Look at illustration B entitled 'Derby Gaol'. It shows George Fox writing in his journal some of the words in the tapestry. Using this and what Alice's mother said, design a poster showing one of the ideals held by the Quakers.

Thinking it through

Think of a time when you or someone you know had to stand up for some ideas when people argued against them and made fun. How did you or they feel?

What advice would you give to somebody else in a similar situation? Would any of Fox's words help?

B A panel from a Quaker tapestry

4 Stacey and the Greek Orthodox Church

About Stacey

Stacey is an English version of a Greek name (Anastasios) linked with Christian belief in the resurrection of Jesus. William, his other name, is after a kind neighbour who helped his grandparents when they came to England from Cyprus.

Has two older brothers, Paul and Leigh, and an older sister, Margarita.

Father runs a fish and chip shop.

Mother works in a greengrocers.

Keen on sports, supports Coventry City, plays rugby at school, indoor football and snooker at a local sports centre.

Also interested in computers, through doing computer studies at school.

Family enjoys walking – they have taken part in sponsored walks for charity.

Goes to a youth club, run by one of his brothers, on Sunday afternoons at church.
This is the Greek Orthodox Church of the Holy Transfiguration.

Stacey

About the Greek Orthodox Church

A Church of the Holy Transfiguration, Coventry

The history of the Greek Orthodox Church goes back to the first Christian leaders or 'apostles', especially St Paul. It survived persecutions under the Roman Emperors until, in the fourth century CE the Emperor Constantine became a Christian himself.

He made his new capital, Constantinople, a Christian city. He called together the bishops of the Church in a 'council' to decide basic beliefs, set out in a 'creed'.

Such councils are called 'ecumenical' because they involved bishops from the whole Christian Church. Seven took place between the fourth and eighth centuries. Loyalty to their decisions is very important for Orthodox Christians.

Misunderstanding and rivalry between the chief bishops, called 'patriarchs', led to a split between Rome and Constantinople. Those Christians loyal to Rome became known as 'Catholics', those loyal to Constantinople continued to call themselves 'Orthodox'.

'We believe in God as the Trinity, so we have Father, Son and Holy Spirit being three different parts, all on the same level, but One. God is a mystery. We can't understand him.' (Stacey's mother) **(1)**

'One of the "saints" went for a walk along the beach where he saw a little boy digging a hole in the sand. The little boy was taking handfuls of water from the sea and putting it in the hole. The saint (he wasn't a saint then!) asked him what he was doing. The boy said, "I'm trying to put all that water into this hole."

The saint looked at the little boy and said, "The water isn't only as far as you can see. It goes further and there are other oceans and other seas."

The little boy looked blank. He obviously didn't understand. I think we're like that child, trying to put God, "the sea" into a little hole, "our minds", and we can't.'   (Stacey's mother) **(2)**

B   Church of the Holy Wisdom (St Sophia), Constantinople, modern Istanbul. (Minarets were added after the Turkish conquest in the fifteenth century)

Making it clear

'Catholic' means 'universal' or 'worldwide'. 'Orthodox' means 'right belief'. It can also mean 'right worship'. 'Creed' comes from the Latin word 'credo' meaning 'I believe.'

Here are some possible reasons for having a 'creed':

- to summarize what Christians believe about God
- to unite as many Christians as possible in one organization
- to resolve differences between different groups of Christians
- to help Christians worship in the same way wherever they are
- to prevent false ideas about God being accepted as Christian
- to explain what Christians believe to non-Christians
- to form a link over the centuries to the first Christians.

Decide on three which you think are most important for Orthodox Christians. Explain your choice to a partner.

Building bridges

In pairs, note down three familiar things which were once mysteries to you but are less mysterious now (for example, how rainbows or snowflakes are formed). Then note down three familiar things which are still mysterious (for example, dreaming, growing up).

Stacey's mother was asked what was distinctive about the Orthodox Church. Part of her answer is given in extract (1).

Which of these beliefs about God could she describe but not understand?

His existence   *What he is like*
How he does things   *His power*
His threefold nature

Explain your choice.

Thinking it through

Extract (2) could be called a 'parable', that is a story with a meaning.

Either Write a parable of your own, perhaps based on an experience you have had, to help someone else understand an important truth about life.

Or Using the idea of a human mind trying to take in huge and mysterious ideas draw a picture, cartoon or diagram to illustrate one of the things which is a mystery to you.

5 Abigail and the Coventry Christian Fellowship

About Abigail

Abigail thinks her parents chose her names because of
   their meanings (Abigail: father have joy; Sarah: princess).
   Both belonged to women whose stories are in the Bible.
Has a younger sister, Lizzie.
Father works part time as an engineer in a water company,
   and part-time as a church leader.
Mother is a music teacher in a secondary school.
Likes music, sings in school choir and youth operetta group. Wants to learn the bass
   guitar. Her real passion is dance, especially ballet. She has three ballet lessons a week.
Plays hockey in school teams. Goes to youth club run by her church on Saturdays.
Family keen on camping and climbing.
Church has no special place of worship. Meets one Sunday a month in a boys' club
   gymnasium and on other Sundays in four different local schools.

Abigail

About the Coventry Christian Fellowship

A   Coventry Boys' Club

The Coventry Christian Fellowship started in 1977 when some Christian families began to meet in each other's houses for worship. It became known as a 'House Church', but numbers became too large to meet in houses. Today it prefers to be called a 'New Church'. Similar churches exist in other places but they aren't part of a national organization or denomination. Abigail's father and another man are co-leaders, jointly responsible for the church.

'One of the distinctive things, which has been quite an attraction, is the style of our worship, particularly the music. We have people within the church, musicians who write songs. New songs are being introduced all the time.
We felt God wanted two particular things of us as a "New Church". One was to send people out, and that has happened. We support work in Africa. We have somebody who's out in central Asia. Our first missionary went to Istanbul.

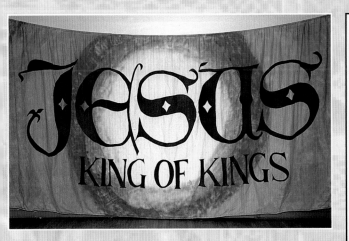

B Banners are hung in the gymnasium when it is used for worship

The other was to bring together the different churches in the city.

My co-leader and I meet regularly with other church leaders. We have lunch together once a month to think and pray about what to do. We aren't stand-offish. We work together with other churches and we don't believe we've got all the answers.

We have another important link with a Christian Fellowship in London.

They have a summer camp every year in which we've been involved.'

(Abigail's father) **(1)**

Making it clear

Place the Church of England, Society of Friends, Greek Orthodox Church and the Coventry Christian Fellowship in historical order beginning with the youngest.

Abigail's father talked about a 'missionary', which means someone 'sent out' to preach and teach people about their religion. For example, Greek Orthodox missionaries originally took Christianity to countries outside the Roman Empire such as Russia.

Looking back over units 2–5, list the places which have sent and received Christian missionaries.

If you don't already know where they are look them up in an atlas.

Building bridges

Think of a time when you had to make a 'fresh start' (for example, moving house, starting in a new form or school).

List two things which you felt were the same as before and two which felt different.

Now look at what this unit tells you about the Coventry Christian Fellowship. List two things they do which are similar to other Christian Churches and two which, they feel, make them different. Compare your findings with a partner.

Working it out

With a partner, draw up a table with three columns. Put one of these headings at the top of each column:
Beliefs   Worship   Organization

Read extract (1). Put a tick in a column whenever Abigail's father mentions one of these things.

Now choose two other denominations from units 2–5, fill in ticks whenever a member of that denomination mentions one of them. Use a different colour for each denomination.

Compare the results for Abigail's church with the others. What do you notice?

Thinking it through

Most of the young people in units 2–5 have a name which they can associate with their religion.

Does your name have a meaning? Why do you think it was chosen?

If you were a parent, how would you choose a name for a new baby? (Remember they will have to live with it!) What sort of things would influence you? Discuss your reasons with a partner.

6 Weekday activities

This unit introduces how being a Christian affects daily life.

A 'normal' day begins

Stacey dislikes getting up early. His Dad gets up at 6.30 to go to work but he doesn't get up until 7.30.

Andrew has his rabbit to feed before school.

Once at school Alice said,

 'I put my lunch in my desk, do any homework I haven't done the night before, then sit around and talk to people, just chat.' **(1)**

Lunchtime

 'I have a packed lunch, then I usually have activities like choir. There's something on every lunchtime. I go to a junior sort of prayer group. It's run by two pupils. We discuss things like the sort of things there are in magazines. Nearer the time we'll do Christmas and Advent and Easter. I do a lot of drama and dance. I'm hoping to take up the bass guitar.' (Abigail) **(2)**

After school

'Mum wants me to work at school, come home, do my homework and go to bed. But my Dad thinks you can't work all the time. He lets you enjoy yourself as well.' (Stacey) **(3)**

Youth organizations

On Tuesdays Andrew goes to 'Campaigners'. They meet at his church.

'It's like Scouts. We wear blue shirts, grey trousers, blue ties and berets. We play games and do badges. I'm doing car maintenance at the moment but you can do pottery, cookery, things like that. There's usually a Bible reading then one of the leaders talks about it.'

On Wednesdays Alice goes to the 'Woodcraft Folk'. They meet at a local school.

'It's a co-operative organization, democratic, for boys and girls. Everyone has a say in what we do. You don't have to wear a uniform but there's a "costume". It's a shirt, quite a deep green. You can put badges on it that you do work for, like citizenship and nature observation. The pioneer badge means you can represent your group anywhere in the world. I've got that.' **(4)**

A Alice's Woodcraft Folk 'pioneer' badge

Making it clear

In pairs, list five things you *have* to do every week and five that you *choose* to do.

Take two of the young people and, from what you have found out so far, put their activities under the same headings. Compare your results with another pair.

As a group, decide which of their activities are the same as other young people and which, if any, they have chosen because they belong to a Christian church.

Building bridges

From your list of things you do every week, choose something that you have to do (for example, get up in the morning).

Decide what makes the difference between times when you're reluctant and times when you're keen to do it.

Now look at the activities you thought were chosen because the young people belonged to a Christian church. What do you think made them keen to go to them?

Bringing God in?

Be constant in the private reading of the Bible and other writings which reveal the ways of God. Make a quiet place wherein you may learn more of the meaning of prayer.
     (*Advices* of the Society of Friends) **(5)**

In every situation seek to be aware of the presence of God.
     (*Advices* of the Society of Friends) **(6)**

Very early next morning he (Jesus) got up and went out. He went away to a remote spot and remained there in prayer. But Simon and his companions went in search of him, and when they found him they said, 'Everybody is looking for you'.
     (*Mark 1:35–7*) **(7)**

B   Getting ready for school

Working it out

Read extracts (5) and (7). The first one is taken from the *Advices* Quakers have to help them. The second is an early incident in one account of Jesus' life.

List some ways in which Christians could try to find time for God in their daily lives.

Thinking it through

Put the title 'Ways of making an ordinary activity special' on a sheet of paper.

Read extracts (3) and (6). Divide your paper into six columns.

Head the left-hand column **Working** and the right-hand one **Leisure**.

With a partner, decide which six of your regular activities (for example, washing up, reading) you'd put under each.

Now write **Helping, Learning, Training** and **Performing** at the top of the other columns. Decide which of the activities could also go under any of these headings.

What difference might it make to the way you feel about it?

7 Reading the Bible: what and why

This unit introduces the Bible and its importance for Christians.

Asked about his hobbies Andrew replied, *'Music and magic'.*

What sort of magic do you do?
'Conjuring. It depends what the audience is like. If there's an adult audience I do more sophisticated tricks.'

What sort of things do you read?
'Magic books, novels, Number One *magazine and* Fast Forward.'

Do you read the Bible?
'Before I go to bed there's One to One. *It's a booklet more geared to my age group. You look up a Bible verse and then say a prayer. Quite often we do* One to One *together as a family, although my Mum and Dad do their own separate ones.'* (Andrew) **(1)**

Making it clear

Opposite is a page from the introduction to *One to One*, a magazine written to help Christians of any denomination read the Bible every day.

The gaps on the shelves show how the books are grouped into sections. The first five books in the Old Testament (called the 'Law') are more important than the others. Then come the 'former' prophets (e.g. Samuel), the 'latter' prophets (e.g. Isaiah) and the 'writings' (i.e. songs and wise sayings). The Old Testament books are all part of the Jewish Bible as well as the Christian Bible.

In the New Testament the four Gospels come first because they are about the life of Jesus. Then come the 'Acts' (of the first Christians, especially St Paul), letters from Paul and others (e.g. Peter) and Revelation (visions about the future).

List the sections to which each of these belong:

John	Ruth
Exodus	James
Daniel	Job

Which of them are also contained in the Jewish Bible?

A Andrew's family studies the Bible with some friends

WHAT IS THE BIBLE?

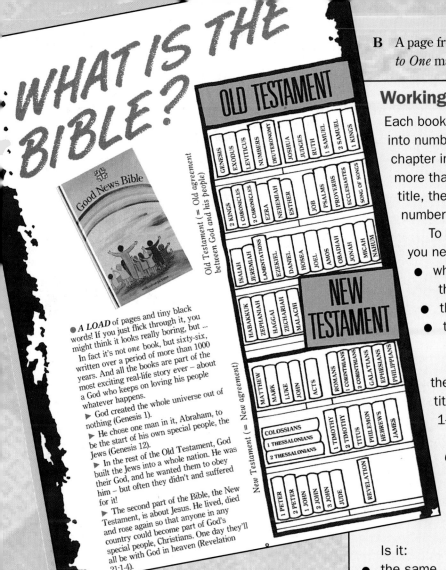

Good News Bible

Old Testament (= Old agreement between God and his people)

New Testament (= New agreement)

OLD TESTAMENT

GENESIS · EXODUS · LEVITICUS · NUMBERS · DEUTERONOMY · JOSHUA · JUDGES · RUTH · 1 SAMUEL · 2 SAMUEL · 1 KINGS

2 KINGS · 1 CHRONICLES · 2 CHRONICLES · EZRA · NEHEMIAH · ESTHER · JOB · PSALMS · PROVERBS · ECCLESIASTES · SONG OF SONGS

ISAIAH · JEREMIAH · LAMENTATIONS · EZEKIEL · DANIEL · HOSEA · JOEL · AMOS · OBADIAH · JONAH · MICAH · NAHUM

HABAKKUK · ZEPHANIAH · HAGGAI · ZECHARIAH · MALACHI

NEW TESTAMENT

MATTHEW · MARK · LUKE · JOHN · ACTS · ROMANS · 1 CORINTHIANS · 2 CORINTHIANS · GALATIANS · EPHESIANS · PHILIPPIANS

COLOSSIANS · 1 THESSALONIANS · 2 THESSALONIANS · 1 TIMOTHY · 2 TIMOTHY · TITUS · PHILEMON · HEBREWS · JAMES

1 PETER · 2 PETER · 1 JOHN · 2 JOHN · 3 JOHN · JUDE · REVELATION

● **A LOAD** of pages and tiny black words! If you just flick through it, you might think it looks really boring, but ...
In fact it's not one book, but sixty-six, written over a period of more than 1000 years. And all the books are part of the most exciting real-life story ever – about a God who keeps on loving his people whatever happens.
▶ God created the whole universe out of nothing (Genesis 1).
▶ He chose one man in it, Abraham, to be the start of his own special people, the Jews (Genesis 12).
▶ In the rest of the Old Testament, God built the Jews into a whole nation. He was their God, and he wanted them to obey him – but often they didn't and suffered for it!
▶ The second part of the Bible, the New Testament, is about Jesus. He lived, died and rose again so that anyone in any country could become part of God's special people, Christians. One day they'll all be with God in heaven (Revelation 21:1-4).

Working it out

Each book in the Bible is divided into numbered chapters and each chapter into verses. If there is more than one book with the same title, the title itself also has a number (e.g. *1 Kings, 2 Peter*).

To look up a Bible reference you need to know:
● where the book comes in the order on the 'shelves'
● the number of the chapter
● the number(s) of the verse(s).

Look up this reference in the Bible: *Revelation* (book title) 21 (chapter number): 1–4 (verse numbers).

The page from *One to One* gives it an 'interpretation' (see first column, last arrow). Check this against the actual words of *Revelation*.

Is it:
● the same
● slightly different
● very different?

Thinking it through

a Andrew reads several books and magazines but the Bible seems to be the only book he reads every day (extract (1)).

Note down some of the things that are so important to you that you try to do them every day (for example, meet up with your best friend).

b Using the evidence you have had so far, write a slogan or design a poster which Christians could use to encourage each other to read the Bible every day.

Building bridges

If you want to check your knowledge or find out more about something, you may need to 'look up a reference' in a book. Which books would you use to find each of the following?
● the capital of a country
● the right spelling of a word
● the meaning of a technical term
● how to get to an address in another town
● how to contact someone on the telephone

According to *One to One* what do Christians hope to find out more about when they look up a Bible reference? Compare your answer with a partner.

8 Reading the Bible: how

This unit looks at some of the ways Christians read the Bible.

What about reading?

'*I always read part of the Bible every day. I'm trying to read all of the Bible.*'

From beginning to end?

'*No! I'm sort of tackling it in chapters because my Dad knows quite a lot about it and he says, "Why don't you read this book?"*'

With Bible reading notes?

'*No, I never seem to be able to stick with those sorts of things and sometimes I just choose things that I want to read. I'm on the Psalms at the moment and I'm reading* The Diary of Anne Frank. *I read two or three Psalms and then I read, say, two of her entries a night.*'

Do you enjoy reading the Psalms?

'*Yes, though some parts are a bit boring.*'

Do you mean they're no longer very good?

'*No! Mostly they almost believed in what Jesus taught but I've been reading some that are mainly saying "Oh God kill our enemies". When Jesus came he taught us not to say things like that.*' (Abigail) **(1)**

(*The Diary of Anne Frank*) **(2)**

> Sunday, 27th September, 1942
>
> Dear Kitty,
> Just had a big bust-up with Mummy for the umpteenth time; we simply don't get on these days and Margot and I don't hit it together these days either. As a rule we don't go in off any too well either. As a rule we don't go in for such outbursts as this in our family. Still, it's by no means always pleasant for me. Margot's and Mummy's nature are completely strange to me. I can understand my friends better than my own mother - too bad!

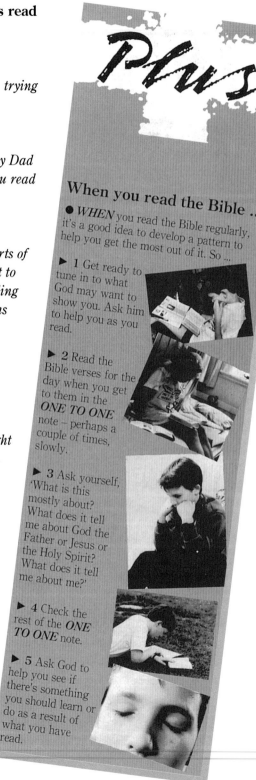

When you read the Bible ...

● *WHEN* you read the Bible regularly, it's a good idea to develop a pattern to help you get the most out of it. So ...

▶ 1 Get ready to tune in to what God may want to show you. Ask him to help you as you read.

▶ 2 Read the Bible verses for the day when you get to them in the *ONE TO ONE* note – perhaps a couple of times, slowly.

▶ 3 Ask yourself, 'What is this mostly about? What does it tell me about God the Father or Jesus or the Holy Spirit? What does it tell me about me?'

▶ 4 Check the rest of the *ONE TO ONE* note.

▶ 5 Ask God to help you see if there's something you should learn or do as a result of what you have read.

A Using notes like *One to One* is Andrew's way of reading the Bible

C Anne Frank in 1940

Making it clear

There is no set pattern which all Christians follow when they read the Bible.

Only two out of several possible ones have been mentioned here.

With a partner, note how much of the Bible Andrew and Abigail are likely to read each day (use this unit and unit 7 for your evidence). Do they each read:

a book   several chapters
one chapter   several verses
a few verses

How does each one choose which Bible passage to read?

Building bridges

With your partner, note down several different types of reading matter, e.g.

novel   reference book
magazine   newspaper
instruction manual   poem

Decide which of the following ways of reading you would choose for each:

- from cover to cover
- picking out the bits I'm interested in
- only what I need for my project.
- carefully, making sure I understand each section
- coming back to it again and again
- skipping unexciting bits but getting to the end.

Which of these approaches might a Christian take to Bible reading?

Explain your choice to another pair.

Working it out

Read the extract from *One to One* (illustration A). In a group, decide what attitude to the Bible it expects its readers to have. Choose two out of the following list, then add one of your own.

- It will give me practical guidance for my daily life.
- It will have a clear and simple message.
- I will need to think carefully in order to understand it.
- I will only understand it if I pray first.
- It will always be interesting.

Now read extract (1). Tick any sentences in your list which fit Abigail's experience. Add another one if you need to.

Thinking it through

Anne Frank was a young Jewish girl. Her diary was written in hiding before the family were deported from Holland by the Nazis during World War II (extract (2)). She died in Belsen concentration camp.

The Psalms are a collection of songs and poems. They plead and argue with God as well as praising and thanking him.

Think of an occasion when (like Anne Frank) you were involved in an argument. Do a drawing to show your feelings or write them down in a few words. Choose a partner you can trust. Show them what you have done without telling them why. Have they ever felt like that?

They may ask you the same question when they show you what they have done.

Now decide whether to tell each other about the actual experience, in confidence.

As a class compare the results. How did those who shared their experiences feel compared with those who kept them to themselves?

Were they more or less confident, or the same as before?

9 Ways of praying: school and home

This unit looks at different situations in which Christians pray.

For all four young people the school day regularly begins with an Assembly.

 'Everyone lines up in their classes and first of all we sing a song. We have hymn books, Mr K says a number and we sing it. Then we have a reading and a prayer and then Mr K reads out the results from sports matches and Mr L reads out who he wants to see in his office. It's normally because you're in trouble!' (Stacey) **(1)**

Prayers sometimes used in school assemblies:

O God, forasmuch as without thee we are not able to please thee;
Mercifully grant that thy Holy Spirit may in all things direct and rule our hearts; through Jesus Christ our Lord. Amen. **(2)**

Lead me from death to life, from falsehood to truth
Lead me from despair to hope, from fear to trust
Lead me from hate to love, from war to peace.
May peace fill our hearts, our world, our universe. **(3)**

 'At mealtimes we say "grace" out loud. We take it in turns.' (Andrew) **(4)**

'Before meals we have a quiet time. We just sit round the table like a small Quaker meeting. We sometimes hold hands. We don't say anything, but I usually think I'm really lucky because so many people haven't anything to eat.' (Alice)

'On Sundays my grandparents sometimes come round for lunch. We say the "Our Father" before we eat. First my father says it, then we all say it together out loud. After we've finished we say another short prayer then we "cross" ourselves afterwards.' (Stacey) **(5)**

'At home, before I go to bed, I say my prayers. I have a book which my Mum gave me. It has two English prayers in it which I like. I also say the Greek prayers that I've got upstairs. One of them is the "Our Father" in Greek and the other is "I believe in one God". The priest says them in church.' (Stacey) **(6)**

Making it clear

a Read extracts (1), (5) and (6) above and unit 6, extracts (5) and (6). Using this evidence rearrange the following list so that the times when Christians are most likely to pray regularly are at the top and the least likely times are at the bottom.
- waking up
- getting dressed
- starting school or work
- having a snack
- playing a game
- telephoning a friend
- having a family meal
- digging the garden
- going to bed

b 'Grace' in extract (4) means a short prayer of thanks for food and drink.
For each family note down an example of thoughts, words or actions which are used in praying.

A Saying 'grace' before a meal

Building bridges

Make a list of the ways in which you remember someone you don't see every day and try to keep in touch (for example, wearing something they gave you, having their photo by your bed).

Look at your list. Which ways seem most important for Christians to remember God?

Working it out

a Extracts (2) and (3) are prayers sometimes used in school assemblies. Decide which of them came from:
- a prayer book for Christian public worship
- a collection of prayers for schools with pupils from several religions.

Explain your reasons to a partner. Which would be easier to memorize?

b In pairs, consider these possible reasons why Christians may want to memorize some prayers and decide which you think might be most important.
- You don't need to carry a book around with you.
- It gives you the words when you don't know what to say.

- You can concentrate better on the meaning of the words.
- It's better for people who can't read.

Explain your reasons to another pair.

c Stacey's two favourite prayers are in English but he and his family say 'Our Father' in Greek. Perhaps because …
- they speak Greek
- it reminds them of their family home in Cyprus
- the New Testament was written in Greek
- it reminds them of the Sunday services in church
- it is the nearest they can get to Jesus' actual words
- they've always done it and don't want to change.

Choose one of these reasons and write down why you chose it. Try it out on a partner. If they chose a different reason, try to decide which is more important.

Thinking it through

On a piece of paper write or draw, anonymously, something you do regularly that makes you feel good (for example, watching the sunset, visiting a relative, listening to music).

On the back write down a single word or phrase to describe your feelings about it.

Write on three other pieces of paper:
a school assembly
b Sunday lunch
c bedtime.

Now write on the back of each how you think Stacey feels about prayers at these times.

In a group, lay out all your pieces of paper face down. Sort them into groups of similar feelings. Turn them over and report your results. Which prayer situations resembled your experiences?

10 What is prayer: a personal link with God?

This unit explores the meaning of prayer for Christians.

For many Christians the 'Our Father', better known in English as the 'Lord's Prayer' (extract (2)), is specially important. In Matthew's Gospel it follows immediately after extract (1) and is part of a whole section containing Jesus' teaching on prayer.

> *When you pray, go into a room by yourself, shut the door, and pray to your Father who is in secret; and your Father who sees what is done in secret will reward you. In your prayers do not go babbling on like the heathen, who imagine that the more they say the more likely they are to be heard. Do not imitate them, for your Father knows your needs before you ask him. This is how you should pray.*
>
> *(Matthew 6:7–8)* **(1)**

The following translation is a modern one used by many churches, including the Church of England.

> *Our Father in heaven*
> *hallowed be your name,*
> *your kingdom come*
> *your will be done,*
> *on earth as in heaven.*
> *Give us today our daily bread*
> *Forgive us our sins*
> *as we forgive those*
> *who sin against us.*
> *Lead us not into temptation*
> *but deliver us from evil.*
> *For the kingdom, the power,*
> *and the glory are yours*
> *now and forever.*
> *Amen.* **(2)**

Making it clear

Which of the following times have been mentioned (in this unit and unit 9) as times when some Christians regularly say the 'Lord's Prayer'?

in a youth club	in Sunday worship
at a party	before a meal
in school assembly	after work
at the shops	before bed

With a partner, think of one reason why this prayer is so important for Christians.

Building bridges

Think of what happened yesterday. Note down anything you were glad about, anything you were sad about and anything you were worried about. Share one of these with a partner. Read 'What is prayer?' (illustration B). Are any of these ideas like your own experience?

A A picture chosen to illustrate a line from the 'Lord's Prayer'

B One of the books of prayers Stacey's mother gave him begins like this

WHAT IS PRAYER?

Prayer is talking with God.

Prayer is praising God for His Goodness.

Prayer is thanking God for His wonderful world.

Prayer is asking God to give us what we need.

Prayer is asking God to help us to understand things that are difficult to understand.

Prayer is telling God our troubles.

Prayer is begging God to forgive us for doing wrong things.

Prayer is a way we meet God.

Prayer is listening to God.

Prayer is doing what God wants.

Prayer is loving God.

Prayer is living with God.

Working it out

Read 'What is prayer?' See if any of the statements apply to a phrase in the Lord's Prayer (extract (2)). If they do, set them out alongside one another. For example, Our Father – talking with God.

Now write down any statements that are left. Choose the one which you think Christians might find easiest and one they might find more difficult. Compare your results with a partner.

Thinking it through

Stacey's prayer book has pictures (called 'icons') as well as words. Choose a picture which helps you concentrate on something true, beautiful or good.

Explain your choice to a partner.

Extension activity

In groups, design an 'Instruction card' for Christians called 'How to pray'.

Draw a diagram to show the thoughts, words, actions and intentions (not necessarily in this order) which you think are essential.

Swap your card with another group.

Use extract (1) to 'test' their result. How successful was it?

11 Sunday worship: Andrew

This unit introduces Christian public worship in the Church of England.

Andrew and his family go to their local Church of England parish church where worship begins at 11 o'clock on a Sunday morning. Each month there is at least one service (or act of worship) called 'Holy Communion' and one called 'Morning Prayer'.

The extract chosen here (extract (1)) comes from the monthly 'Family Worship'. Young people stay with the adult congregation for the whole of this service. On other occasions they leave part way through for their own separate activities.

Andrew is part of a music group which accompanies the singing. After the section called the 'Creed' there are Bible readings, a talk and more hymns and prayers.

Making it clear

Read the extract from 'Family Worship' (opposite). Use the photographs to help you note down where in the service the congregation might join in and decide how much they are helped by the way the worship is ordered. Choose from the following.

not at all	*very little*
now and again	*quite a lot*
a great deal	*as much as possible*

A A congregation singing hymns

B A church music group

24

An extract from
'Family Worship' **(1)**

FAMILY WORSHIP

WELCOME

Minister: In God's presence we have gathered together as his family, and we have come to give him praise.

All: **Help us, Lord, to praise you.**

Minister: To hear what he wants to teach us through the Bible.

All: **Help us, Lord, to learn from you.**

Minister: To pray to him about the needs of the world.

All: **Help us. Lord, to pray to you.**

Minister: To ask him to forgive our sins.

All: **Help us, Lord, to be truly sorry.**

Minister: And to enjoy the friendship of our brothers and sisters in Christ.

All: **Help us, Lord, to love each other.**

Minister: Let us shout for joy to the Lord who loves us.

All: **Great is the Lord and most worthy of praise!**

Hymn 1

NOTICES

PRAYER

Minister: Now is the time to turn to God and seek his mercy, for we have strayed from his ways like lost sheep, but like a good shepherd he has sought us and saved us, and longs to forgive our sins.

Minister: For the actions which have angered you, we are truly sorry,

All: **In your mercy, Lord, forgive us.**

Minister: For the words which have wounded you, we are truly sorry,

All: **In your mercy, Lord, forgive us.**

Minister: For the thoughts which have betrayed you. we are truly sorry,

All: **In your mercy, Lord, forgive us.**

Minister: For the failures which have let you down, we are truly sorry,

All: **In your mercy, Lord, forgive us.**

Minister: Almighty God, who forgives all who truly repent, have mercy upon us, pardon and deliver us from all our sins, confirm and strengthen us in all goodness, and keep us in life eternal; through Jesus Christ our Lord. Amen.

Minister: Give thanks to the Lord, because he is good.

All: **His love goes on forever.**

Minister: Sing a new song to the Lord.

All: **He has done wonderful things.**

Songs

CREED

Minister: Do you believe and trust in God the Father, who made the world?

All: **I believe and trust in him.**

Minister: Do you believe and trust in his Son, Jesus Christ, who redeemed mankind?

All: **I believe and trust in him.**

Minister: Do you believe and trust in his Holy Spirit, who gives life to the people of God?

All: **I believe and trust in him.**

Minister: This is the faith of the church.

All: **This is our faith. We believe and trust in one God, Father, Son and Holy Spirit.**

Building bridges

With a partner, decide which of the following experiences of music is most enjoyable:

● humming a tune on your own
● listening to a tape
● attending a live concert
● performing together in a group.

Now look at the photographs. Which musical experiences are they most like?

Can you think of a reason for using this style of worship?

Working it out

For Christians worship is a two-way process. The worshippers offer something to God, and they believe that, in a mysterious but real way, God offers them something in return.

From extract (1), and the summary of what follows it, write down two occasions where something is offered to God and two where the worshippers expect to receive something from him. Compare your list with a partner.

12 *Sunday worship: Stacey*

This unit introduces worship in the Orthodox tradition.

Worship for Stacey and his family begins at 11 o'clock in the Greek Orthodox Church of the Holy Transfiguration, but not all the congregation will be there from the beginning. The worship, called the 'Divine Liturgy', can last almost three hours.

A A priest reading the Gospel

Stacey is an altar boy.

'I go into the "holy bit" behind the screen, the sanctuary where the priest and the altar are. The priest has a Bible reading. He reads in Greek and then my Mum, who sings, reads it in English. Sometimes another altar boy reads out of the Bible and I read the "I believe in one God" and my cousin reads the "Our Father". Then the priest has a speech at the end, taking note of the Bible story. It's in Greek, something like a moral, and he tells the story too, elaborating it.' (Stacey) **(1)**

Stacey's mother reading the Bible 'lesson' is the only time when English is used in the Liturgy. As a leading singer in the choir she plays an essential part in the worship. The whole Liturgy is sung, unaccompanied, from start to finish. Often the choir will sing an anthem while the priest chants a prayer in the sanctuary.

The high point of the worship is the consecration of the bread and wine on the altar, using words spoken by Jesus at the 'Last Supper' (e.g. *Matthew 26:26–8*).

Before this there are processions in which the priest is accompanied by the altar boys carrying lights and banners. One (holding the Gospels) represents the coming of Jesus into the world, another (carrying the bread and wine) his death and burial.

In the Divine Liturgy our Lord is present: first in the person of His priest, secondly, in His Word which is read in the Church, and thirdly according to His promise: 'where two or three are gathered in My name, there am I in the midst of them' (Matthew 18:20). Lastly He is really and truly present upon the altar under the appearances of consecrated Bread and Wine.

(The Divine Liturgy Explained) **(2)**

B Altar boy swinging a censer during the procession

Working it out

a Read extracts (1) and (2). Write down any ways in which you think Stacey and the other altar boys help to bring the worshippers into the presence of God. List your findings under the headings 'words' and 'actions'.

b Before the end of the Liturgy those who are specially prepared come forward to receive 'Holy Communion' (the consecrated bread and wine) from the priest.

From photograph C and extract (2) write down how you think a person might feel about this part of the service. Explain your answer to a partner.

Making it clear

Using the information and photographs write down which of the following you would normally find in Orthodox worship.

incense   hymn books   pictures
vestments   guitars   candles
anthems   chalice-cup

Add any other important items not included in this list.

Look at photograph B. What is the priest carrying? Why do you think he is stooping and the congregation are bowing their heads?

Building bridges

In pairs, list five to ten ways of making an occasion special (e.g. flowers, best clothes).

Now list as many ways as you can in which such 'special' things find a place in the Orthodox Liturgy. As a result of your findings complete the following sentence:

Orthodox Christians are made aware of God's presence in their worship by ...

Check how many of the five senses have been included in your answer.

C   The priest uses a spoon to give Holy Communion

Thinking it through

This unit has given you some idea of how important the senses are in the Orthodox tradition. Choose one item from the list below which appeals to you and write a short poem or design a poster showing what you feel about it.

● shining colours; gold, silver, crimson
● candles glowing in the dark
● walking in a procession with banners
● hearing a choir singing
● the scent of incense
● gestures of reverence and devotion
● familiar words, a prayer or saying
● any other sight or sound which means a lot to you

13 Sunday worship: Abigail

This unit introduces worship in a 'New Church' tradition.

Abigail's Sunday followed a slightly different pattern from the others. When she was interviewed the Christian Fellowship had been forced to change the time of their worship because their normal meeting place, the gymnasium of a boys' club, was being redecorated after a fire.

'Church isn't until three o'clock so I usually help Mum make the lunch. We're doing an activity book in our young people's group, so I usually end up doing that in the morning, then go off to church after lunch.

At church we have about half an hour to an hour's praise and worship, then the children and young people go off into groups.

We do quite a lot of discussing and there's a test at the end of each topic, just to make sure we've got the gist of what we're doing. There's a verse from the Bible, to do with the chapter we've been studying, which we memorize.

Sometimes we come back into the main session just to sing one song, sometimes we stay for the whole time. Usually it's just someone preaching but sometimes there is the special occasion like last week. There was a child whom the doctors said couldn't be born and it was born. It was obviously a miracle and there was a special thanksgiving for the baby. We stayed in for that.' (Abigail) **(1)**

'I love worshipping God, I just love it. I like seeing my friends, and I really enjoy it.'

Do you dance as well as sing?
'Yes. Actually I'm a bit shy. I don't usually get up and dance in front of the whole church. But sometimes – it's a bit hard to describe it – loads of people get up and dance. You just dance because the song is so joyful and you're very happy and you just dance! Maybe God does sometimes tell everybody to get up and dance.'

Is it a different kind of dance from ballet?
'Yes! Most people who dance aren't dancers. It's no particular kind of dance. It's just what everybody can do freely and enjoy doing.' **(2)**

A Dance as a part of worship

B A music group leading worship

C   Putting up banners before worship

It's so good to know You,
Who is like unto You?
You have given us life,
Made us alive in Jesus by Your Spirit.
In You there is life and
Darkness cannot hide
Your glory and Your light
O Lord ... of heaven and earth.
Chorus: *Lead us on*
             Father renew
             A deep love for You.
             Set our hearts on fire again
             Fan the flame
             In hearts that are cold
             That our love may grow
             Stronger every day.
         (Part of a song written by Steve Kelly,
a member of the Christian Fellowship) **(3)**

Making it clear

Here are some of the things Abigail said
she did at church.

Bible study   meeting friends
singing   hearing preaching
dancing   group discussions
thanksgiving

     Re-order them, starting with the
things you think she enjoys most.

Building bridges

In groups, think of some of
the things you can do in an
open space (for example,
games, drama) and the
props you would need to
create the right
atmosphere for each.
Your next task is to make
a gymnasium into a place
of worship. Using the
photographs as well as
your own ideas, list some ways in
which this could be done.

     Make your plan into a diagram
showing how you would create a
feeling of fellowship (togetherness).
Remember that you will need to use
things which can be put in place and
removed again quickly.

Working it out

Worship at the Christian Fellowship
doesn't have a set form. The leaders
of the Church follow the guidance they
feel God is giving them each week.
Songs, prayers, Bible readings and
preaching all take place along with
contributions from members of the
congregation who have particular
experiences they wish to share. Read
extracts (2) and (3).

     List three feelings which this
worship tries particularly to encourage.
With a partner, decide which activities
mentioned in this unit would be most
likely to help a worshipper feel this way.

14 Sunday worship: Alice

This unit introduces worship in the Quaker tradition.

'We're a Quaker family and on Sundays we go to "Meeting". The Meeting House is in Hill Street. Before Meeting I meet up with my friends there. There's a group of about twelve of us who are aged from about 13 to 16. Anyway I meet up with them and then we go into Meeting.

We sit down. We're kind of vaguely in a circle. We sit all round. We don't sit in a block with someone at the front talking to us. And we have a table in the middle. It's called "waiting upon God".

Sometimes you just feel that everybody's together. You get a feeling of love. We usually go out after about a quarter of an hour. Sometimes we stay in, maybe once a month. It's about an hour long or an hour and a quarter.' (Alice) **(1)**

The Quaker Meeting may remain in silence for a whole hour 'waiting on God' but this is unusual. As Alice's mother explained,

'Spoken ministry, such as a prayer or some words may arise from anyone present.' **(2)**

Do you come faithfully to meeting for worship, with heart and mind prepared? Do you seek to know communion with the Holy Spirit in your midst?

Are you sensitive to one another's needs and to God's promptings, whether your response be in silence or through the spoken word?

(*Queries* of the Society of Friends) **(3)**

Silence is simply a preparation for being still, the means of worship not the worship itself. Stillness is enhanced when experienced in the company of others. This is why Friends meet for worship. The practice of stillness needs guidance and nourishment, for we are not self-sufficient.

(John Punshon, *Encounter with Silence*) **(4)**

A A Quaker Meeting for Worship

Making it clear

Which of the following has been mentioned as typical of a Quaker Meeting for Worship?
- sitting in rows
- singing hymns
- having a table in the middle
- sitting in a circle
- a brief talk
- someone leading from the front
- silently 'waiting on God'
- spoken prayers

Arrange the ideas you have chosen in the order you think a Quaker might, with the most important first.

Building bridges

Mime to a partner the following experiences of 'waiting' without saying which experience you are acting out. Choose your own order.
- Your friend is coming on the next train.
- You are in the doctor's surgery.
- You are waiting for the lesson to end.

How were they able to tell which was which?

Look at photograph A of the Quaker Meeting for Worship. What sort of feelings do you think they might have about 'waiting on God'?

Working it out

From what you have learned in units 11–13, in pairs, note down some of the ways in which Christians offer worship to God. What do extracts (3) and (4) in this unit add to your list? Try to explain to another pair why these are particularly important to Quakers.

Thinking it through

This is an optional exercise, to be used with discretion, for which students will need to be fully prepared.

First try to be silent on your own for up to five minutes.

If you haven't already had this experience, in a small group allow yourself to be led through a 'stilling' exercise. Write down what you felt about each experience.

Which did you find was the hardest to concentrate on?

What further advice would you want to add to extract (4)?

B The title panel from a Quaker tapestry

THE RELIGIOUS SOCIETY of FRIENDS "might be thought of as a prism through which the DIVINE LIGHT passes to become visible in a spectrum of many colours, many more in their richness than words alone can express." Faith + Practice

15 Christmas and Epiphany

This unit explores links between two Christian festivals.

 'The times of the year I enjoy most are Christmas, Easter and my birthday.'

What do you do for Christmas?

'Mostly like everybody else, putting decorations round the house, pulling crackers, things like that – although we go to church on Christmas Day.'

(Andrew) **(1)**

A Andrew opens his Christmas presents

What is your favourite festival?

 'It ought to be Easter really but I enjoy Christmas more. I suppose some of it's to do with the less religious side, like having family visiting, giving and getting presents. But it's got an atmosphere. It's obviously when Jesus was born, and celebrating his birthday, when he first entered the world. It's almost like a miracle really, the wise men and the shepherds coming to see him. It's just all very exciting and I love it.' (Abigail) **(2)**

On Christmas Day, in Andrew's church, the Bible reading will be the beginning of the Gospel of John. It includes these words:

There appeared a man named John. He was sent from God, and came as a witness to testify to the light...
The true light which gives light to everyone was even then coming into the world.
He was in the world; but the world, though it owed its being to him, did not recognize him.
He came to his own and his own people would not accept him.
But to all who did accept him, to those who put their trust in him, he gave the right to become children of God...
So the Word became flesh; he made his home among us, and we saw his glory, such glory as befits the Father's only Son, full of grace and truth. (John 1:6–14) **(3)**

Christmas decorations go up in shops and city streets well before Christmas Eve. The traditional day for them to come down is Twelfth Night, the evening before Epiphany. This Greek word means an 'appearance'. Many Christians use it to describe 6 January.

On this day some Churches, including the Church of England, remember the story of the Wise Men. Others, particularly the Orthodox, celebrate the baptism of Jesus. Mark's Gospel begins with this:

> *John the Baptist appeared in the wilderness proclaiming a baptism in token of repentance, ... and everyone flocked to him from the countryside ... and the city of Jerusalem, and they were baptized by him in the river Jordan, confessing their sins ... It was at this time that Jesus came from Nazareth ... and was baptized in the Jordan by John. As he was coming up out of the water, he saw the heavens break open and the Spirit descend on him, like a dove. And a voice came from heaven: 'You are my beloved Son; in you I take delight.'* (Mark 1:4–11) **(4)**

In Stacey's church there is a special ceremony in which the priest blesses the water which will be used at baptisms, sprinkling it also on the congregation. He then visits their homes to give them a blessing for the coming year.

> *'At Epiphany, in the villages in Cyprus, the priest would go round and bless every house.'*
>
> (Stacey's mother) **(5)**

B Epiphany service in the Greek Orthodox Church

Building bridges

With a partner, plan a celebration for an event you think is important (for example, New Year). List the things you might need and what you might do.

Compare your list with what Andrew and Abigail say about Christmas in extracts (1) and (2).

Why do you think so many different things happen to celebrate Jesus' birthday?

Working it out

John and Mark do not begin their Gospels with a Nativity (birth) story – see extracts (3) and (4). Here are some possible reasons. Arrange them in the order of importance you think a Christian might choose.

● They didn't know the stories.
● They wanted to remind people that Jesus grew up.
● They felt people sentimentalized Christmas.
● They thought of Jesus as Son of God not a baby in a manger.
● They wanted to concentrate on what Jesus did as a man.

Using the information in extracts (3) and (4) give two reasons why John the Baptist is important for Christians.

Thinking it through

In a group, write down on separate cards or pieces of paper any words you link with the idea of 'God' (e.g. almighty, eternal). Put them to one side.

Read extracts (3) and (4). On separate cards list the images their writers link with Jesus (e.g. light, word). Turn up both sets of cards. Are any the same?

Individually, choose a card from either set. Write or draw what this image means for you. Compare your results.

16 Lent and Easter

This unit explores the meanings of the most important Christian festival.

After Jesus' Baptism, Mark's Gospel says:

> *At once the Spirit drove him out into the wilderness, and there he remained for forty days tempted by Satan.*
> *(Mark 1:12–13)* **(1)**

Christians call this period 'Lent' and make it a time of penitence. For many centuries Easter was the only time when converts to Christianity were baptized. Before this they learnt about their faith and kept forty days of 'fasting' as a personal discipline.

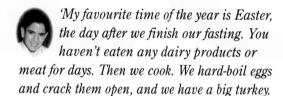

> *'My favourite time of the year is Easter, the day after we finish our fasting. You haven't eaten any dairy products or meat for days. Then we cook. We hard-boil eggs and crack them open, and we have a big turkey.*
> *Easter is more important than Christmas, because that's when Christ died and rose again. We go to church every day for a week and then, on Saturday night, we go to church at midnight and it goes on till about three in the morning.'* (Stacey) **(2)**

During 'Holy Week' (the week before Easter) Christians commemorate the last week of Jesus' life:
- His entry into Jerusalem on Palm Sunday
- His Last Supper with his disciples, followed by his betrayal and arrest in the garden of Gethsemane, on Maundy Thursday.

On Good Friday Andrew and Stacey each attend services which recall the trial, crucifixion, death and burial of Jesus.

Andrew's service is in the morning and includes a procession round the church, stopping at each of the stained glass windows depicting one of these events, for a reading from the Gospels and prayers.

It is true — the Lord has risen

A An Easter banner in Christ Church

At Stacey's church the midday service includes a ceremony at which the figure of Jesus is taken down from the cross and wrapped in white linen.

The evening service ends with a procession carrying the icon of the dead Christ, woven on cloth, round the outside of the church before it is brought back inside and placed in a specially constructed sepulchre decorated with flowers.

The icon is sprinkled with myrrh by the priest and then covered with flower petals by the young girls of the church, who represent the role of the women in the burial of Jesus.

B The sepulchre at a Greek Orthodox Good Friday service

In addition to what individual churches do during Holy Week there are often ecumenical activities involving Christians of several denominations.

Abigail and her family joined many others for the Easter Vigil in Coventry Cathedral. This begins on the Saturday night and continues until just after dawn on Easter Sunday. It is meant for Christians 'aged from 14 to 104' but Abigail's mother rang up and persuaded them to admit two 'responsible 13-year-olds'.

Making it clear

Match these main events to the following days:
- Palm Sunday
- Maundy Thursday
- Good Friday
- Easter Saturday
- Easter Sunday
- ☐ The Last Supper
- ☐ Jesus is buried
- ☐ Jesus rides into Jerusalem
- ☐ Jesus arrested in Gethsemane
- ☐ Jesus' trials
- ☐ The empty tomb
- ☐ The crucifixion
- ☐ Jesus' tomb guarded

Building bridges

Think of an occasion when you had to tell someone some bad news, or when you had to face some yourself. Tell a partner how you felt. Help them share their own 'bad news' experience with you. What feelings did you have in common?

Write down three feelings you think Christians might have when they hear what happened to Jesus in Holy Week.

Working it out

In groups, think of three main reasons why Christians seem to concentrate on Jesus' death rather than his resurrection around Easter time. Here are some suggestions to add to your own.
- They feel sorry for him, suffering so much pain.
- They want to show their personal devotion to him.
- It helps them cope with their own suffering and disappointments.
- The gospels give more details about the last week of Jesus' life than all the rest.
- The way people treated Jesus helps them see their own faults and failures and ask God's forgiveness for them.
- Resurrection is a mystery but death is something they all understand.

Thinking it through

The services mentioned in this unit include time for reflection, to think about the events described in the Gospels and how people can learn from them today.

Think of an event which you feel taught you something. Describe what you learnt from it, in note form for yourself.

17 Other special occasions in the year

This unit explores the place of religion in birthdays and holidays.

Alice has not been mentioned for a few pages because Quakers don't have the same approach to traditional festivals as other Christians. You'll find out later what she enjoys most (unit 27).

All the young people said they enjoyed their birthdays.

Like the others Stacey gets cards and presents but he has an additional 'name day' ceremony as a part of the church service.

Each Orthodox boy and girl has a name connected with a saint. The day on which that saint is specially remembered in the Church becomes that person's name day. It's usually quite different from their birthday but equally important.

A Stacey's 'name day' icon

'We have special saints' days for each name. Each person has a saint's day. On the Sunday after it you get your icon, the icon with "your" saint on it. There's a table in the middle, near the altar. It's got five loaves of bread on it. You walk round the table with the priest holding the icon, and the priest sings. If it's several people's saint's day, say if you had a name like John, then you'd all hold the icon. Then the priest gives you the bread, you cut it and give it to everybody as they're walking out from the church.'

(Stacey) **(1)**

Summer holidays are also different for Stacey. He helps his father three days a week in the fish and chip shop. But the family also manages to afford a visit to Cyprus every few years. Here he sees several of his relatives. He also visits some of the Christian places of pilgrimage on the island. Many of them are monasteries.

Abigail's mother described one of the things they do in the summer.

'One thing we try to do for the 10- to 25-year-olds is to have a holiday week. So, as a church, we run two separate weeks in North Wales. One is for 10 to 13 and is – sort of – outdoor pursuits. We go to a cottage which only sleeps about thirteen. We hire another cottage in the village as well so that if there are families they're not all crammed in too close together for a week!

B Abigail in North Wales

There is a specifically "spiritual" content in the evening, but we look upon the whole thing as spiritual. Struggling up a mountain can have as much spiritual value for people as Bible study in the evening.'

(Abigail's mother) **(2)**

Andrew's interest in conjuring gives him something else to look forward to. He's almost old enough to join an organization called 'The Fellowship of Christian Magicians, Europe'. He hopes to go to their annual conference in the autumn to meet other conjurers, learn new 'magic' acts and find out how they use conjuring to promote their Christian beliefs.

C Andrew's 'magic' kit

Making it clear

Most young people look forward to their birthdays and summer holidays.

Which of the following ways were used by the young Christians in this unit to bring God into these activities?

- party for young handicapped people
- name day ceremony in church
- priest blesses birthday cake
- visiting pilgrimage sites
- Christian arts festival
- Church-organized outdoor pursuits
- Christian youth camp
- Christian magicians' conference

Building bridges

Think of an occasion when you succeeded for the first time in doing something you found difficult (e.g. swimming a length). How did you feel afterwards? Choose from the following.

relieved   frightened   more confident determined to do even better keen to try again

Tell a partner what you think the experience taught you about yourself. Would it have been different if everything had been easy?

What do you think Abigail might learn from rock climbing in Wales?

Working it out

Read extract (1). Stacey's icon (illustration A) shows an event, celebrated on 14 September, not an individual saint. It records the story of how Helena, mother of the Emperor Constantine, found part of the cross on which Jesus died. The icon shows it being held up in public. Helena made gifts to the church in Cyprus on her way back from her pilgrimage to Jerusalem.

Using the information in this and previous units give one or more reasons why you think Stacey's mother chose this particular name day for him. Share your answers.

Thinking it through

Using extract (2) and any similar experiences you may have had, write an entry for your diary of a typical day on an 'outdoor pursuits' holiday, including the chores!

In a group, decide how any of these activities could have a 'spiritual value' (i.e. building up your personality and character).

18 People and ideas which influence us

This unit introduces how important beliefs are for Christians.

Where do we get our personal picture of the world from?

Here are some of the influences mentioned by the four young people.

All their families took a daily newspaper, in most cases the local *Evening Telegraph*. Only Alice's family had any religious magazines. They got the Quaker weekly, called *The Friend*, which Alice also read.

They were all allowed to watch what they liked on TV, so long as it wasn't on too late. They regularly watched the early evening 'soap' when they got in from school. Andrew preferred magic shows.

They were asked about parents.

'I'm very much influenced by what they say,' said Abigail.

What about friends? Andrew said, *'If they were doing something you'd want to join in.'*

How do we fit new ideas and experiences into this picture?

In this extract Abigail explains why she gives to charities.

'I'm quite often influenced by the Church. Maybe more from the Church and from television. Sometimes when there's trouble in the world people from the Church go out to those countries. We've got a few friends who have done that. Then there
are things on TV that really make you think. For example, you feel a lot more like going and buying recycled products.' (Abigail) **(1)**

But is there anything in Christian teaching about recycling and 'Third World' issues?

'I think there is. Jesus encouraged people to give away their money and property to the poor and that was charity. He also taught that you shouldn't be greedy. God made the world so we shouldn't waste it. We've got technology so we can know when a disaster is going to occur. God gave us the world so, if it's being destroyed, we should do something about it. He gave us it. We shouldn't want to lose it.' (Abigail) **(2)**

Making it clear

Using the information on this page and what you can find out from units 6, 7, 9 and 11–14 write a checklist of all the influences mentioned so far (for example, parents, TV).

Put a tick against any item if you think the same thing also influences you.

Number, in order of importance, which six things you think will have most influence on a Christian's picture of the world (for example, Bible study).

Compare your results with a partner. Can you agree? Write down your reasons for your decisions.

Building bridges

In groups, choose an issue on which there is some disagreement (e.g. putting animals in a zoo). Write down where each side gets its ideas from. Decide what or who might make you change your mind. Compare your answers with Abigail's (extract (1)).

Working it out

a Read the Christian Aid statement (B).

Write down any reasons for helping the 'Third World' which it adds to Abigail's (extract (2)).

List the ideas they share and the 'authority' (reasons) given for them. (e.g. Jesus' example).

Is Abigail's answer:
- the same
- very similar
- rather different
- very different?

b Choose a partner. Write two captions to replace the one in the signboard in the Calman cartoon. One should use Abigail's argument and the other the *Christian Aid* statement.

Compare the two. Which would you choose to go on a T-shirt for Christian Aid?

A   Cartoon by Calman

Thinking it through

Christians seem to have certain 'reference points' or 'authorities' to turn to when they face new or challenging situations.

Conduct a survey of the 'authorities' people in the class rely on in their lives.

Choose one of the following issues.

6

HOW is Christian Aid Christian

Christian Aid is Christian because:

- **Christian faith provides the REASON for caring. Christians believe that God loves the world and all that is in it. They believe that God became a human in Jesus and that in a real sense they can meet God in every human being.**

- **Christian faith provides the EXAMPLE of Jesus and how he mixed with and respected those who were poor or despised by others.**

- **Christian faith provides TEACHING. The Old Testament makes powerful statements about justice and Jesus adds to these in his own teaching. Ever since New Testament times, Christians have been committed to living out Jesus's teaching on how people should regard and treat the poor.**

- **Christian faith provides a VISION of the kingdom of God. This shows what the world could be like. It also gives meaning to life which goes beyond our present experiences. This vision includes forgiveness and reconciliation.**

- **In a practical sense Christian Aid is Christian because it was set up by the churches of the UK and Ireland to put into ACTION the concern of Christians for those in need. This concern is for all, whatever their race or faith.**

B   Part of a Christian Aid leaflet

- Have we a special place in the universe? **or**
- How should we use our scientific knowledge?

In groups, write down anonymously where each person would go for an answer. Exchange your group's results with another group for analysis.

First list them under general headings such as:

TV documentaries	*teachers*
magazines	*parents*

Then write down why you think they were chosen.

What gave them 'authority' on these issues?

Report your results and compare them across the class.

19 Christian beliefs: Creation

In this unit we begin to examine some important Christian beliefs.

We start by exploring what Christians think about the world we live in.

We find ourselves in a bewildering world. We want to make sense of what we see around us and to ask: What is the nature of the universe? What is our place in it and where did it and we come from? Why is it the way it is? (Prof. Stephen Hawking, *A Brief History of Time*) **(1)**

A The Andromeda galaxy

'God made the world, so we shouldn't waste it. He gave us it. We shouldn't want to lose it.' (Abigail) **(2)**

We believe in one God, the Father, the Almighty, maker of heaven and earth, of all that is, seen or unseen.
(*Nicene Creed*, 325 CE, as adapted in the Alternative Service Book of the Church of England) **(3)**

In the beginning God created the heavens and the earth. The earth was a vast waste, darkness covered the deep, and the spirit of God hovered over the surface of the water. God said, 'Let there be light,' and there was light, and God saw the light was good and he separated light from darkness. (Genesis 1:1–4) **(4)**

By faith we understand that the universe was formed by God's command, so that the visible came forth from the invisible. (Hebrews 11:1) **(5)**

The works of the Lord are great, sought out of all them that have pleasure therein.
(*Psalm 111:2*, inscribed above the entrance to the Cavendish Laboratory, Cambridge where discoveries about electricity, nuclear energy and the structure of DNA were made) **(6)**

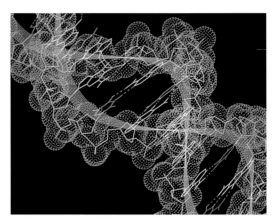

B A computer representation of a DNA molecule

'I have spent most of my working life as a theoretical physicist. All my life I have been a member of the worshipping and believing community of the Church and for the last eleven years I have been an Anglican priest. Consequently I am someone who wants to take both science and theology seriously.'
(Dr John Polkinghorne) **(7)**

When asked: What did God do before he created the universe? Augustine didn't reply: He was preparing hell for people who ask such questions. Instead, he said that time was a property of the universe that God created, and that time did not exist before the beginning of the universe. (Prof. Stephen Hawking, *A Brief History of Time*) **(8)**

Augustine, mentioned in the above extract, was an African bishop who lived in the fourth century.

'We now know that the universe has had a history. Far from the world as we experience it having come into being almost instantaneously and "ready made", it was once very different from the way it is today. Its many-billion-year history ... will discourage any thought of a creator that works by magic. He is not a God in a hurry.' (Dr John Polkinghorne) **(9)**

Making it clear

To answer the questions in extract (1) Christians often refer to three 'authorities':

Scripture – the text of the Bible
Tradition – Christian teaching and customs from earlier centuries (e.g. creeds)
Reason – using all the knowledge you have now.

Draw up a table with each of these authorities as the heading of a column. Look at extracts (2)–(8). Put the number of each extract in the column which it seems to fit best.

Compare your answers with a partner. What reasons are there for any differences between them? (For example, some may fit into more than one column.)

Building bridges

In groups write down five aspects of the world which you think are:

a alien, hostile, terrifying
b mysterious, unpredictable
c good, reliable.

Which would you choose as a subject for:

1 a science fiction story
2 a song for Christian worship
3 a scientific investigation?

Explain your choices to another group.

Working it out

Belief in Creation helps Christians answer two rather different questions:

a What sort of God created the universe?
b What sort of universe did God create?

In pairs, decide which question seems most important in extracts (3)–(5) and (7)–(9). Which do you think best answers the questions in extract (1)? Compare your results.

Thinking it through

a In pairs, note down three things about the natural world on which you each have strong feelings. What makes you feel this way?

Why do you think Abigail feels so strongly about her belief (extract (2))? Do her ideas about God or her ideas about the world have anything in common with yours?

b Think of an occasion when you created something.

Write three words which describe your feelings about the experience.

Talk about it to a partner and share their experience of creation.

Which of your words might a Christian want to put into a song about God creating the universe?

This unit explores one of the central beliefs of Christianity.

What's special about being a Christian?

'It's quite different from non-believers because you believe in life after death, in Jesus, God and the Holy Spirit. You believe in the kingdom of God.'

What distinguishes Christians from others?

'We believe that Christ came, we believe that he is the Son of God, he died to take away our sins.' (Abigail) **(1)**

We believe in one Lord, Jesus Christ, the only Son of God …
For us men and for our salvation he came down from heaven;
by the power of the Holy Spirit he became incarnate of the Virgin Mary
and was made man.
For our sake he was crucified under Pontius Pilate;
He suffered death and was buried.
On the third day he rose again in accordance with the Scriptures.

(Part of the *Nicene Creed*) **(2)**

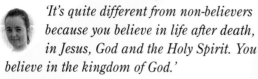

God was in Christ reconciling the world to himself, no longer holding people's misdeeds against them.

(*2 Corinthians 5:19*) **(3)**

God so loved the world that he gave his only Son, that everyone who has faith in him may not perish but have eternal life. It was not to judge the world that God sent his Son into the world, but that through him the world might be saved.

(*John 3:16–17*) **(4)**

Making it clear

Read extracts (1)–(4). Each gives a brief summary of the heart of Christian belief. Which of the following phrases describes what Christians think is happening to them?
● being judged
● entering the kingdom of God
● being condemned
● having their sins taken away
● perishing
● being saved
● being reconciled to God

Building bridges

Think of something you wish you hadn't done, even if you 'got away with it'. What makes you unhappy about it?
● I hurt somebody.
● I let myself down.
● I didn't realize what would happen.
● I couldn't help myself.
● Any other reason.

Write down what you wish would happen if you could go back and start again. How do you feel now?

What word or phrase from extracts (1)–(4) could show that Christians believe something like that has happened to them?

For Christians salvation (being 'saved') involves having their sins taken away.

'Sin' can mean evils, like robbery and murder, chosen deliberately. But it can also mean any failure to live up to God's purpose for humanity. It involves attitudes as well as actions.

These can form a barrier separating humanity from God, making people reject God's love.

For Christians sin is not so much a choice as a condition. Like a disease it effects good people as well as evil ones. It can take hold of groups and societies as well as individuals.

Coventry Cathedral symbolizes this belief. The original one was burnt down during World War II, when a German air raid targeted the city. Two charred timbers from the old cathedral form a cross within the ruins. Behind it are carved the words 'Father forgive', spoken by Jesus at his crucifixion.

Inside the new cathedral, built beside the ruins of the old, are gifts from other cities which suffered similar destruction, including Dresden, bombed by the British in revenge. **(5)**

A 'Crucifixion', part of Graham Sutherland's tapestry in Coventry Cathedral

Working it out

Write or draw something which makes you angry because it causes suffering. Swap your ideas with a partner. Can anything change these situations for the better?

Read extract (5) and look at the photograph. Why do you think Christians chose these images to express their feelings about suffering?

Thinking it through

Christians often turn to St Paul's letters (extract (3)) when trying to understand what God has done for them because Paul, a former persecutor of the Christians, wrote from his own experience of salvation. Even he had to stretch words beyond their normal meaning as there was no simple way of explaining what had happened.

Think of any experience you have had in which something that seemed to be bad turned out to be good (for example, losing your way but meeting someone who helped you get home safely). Write down a word or phrase to explain how you felt. Show it to a partner. Now share your experience with them. Decide which of these gave them the best understanding of the experience. Share your results with another pair.

The first Christians found that they, too, had to tell a story. This is why they wrote the Gospels, good news about how something which seemed to be bad turned out to be good. What Jesus said and did showed that God had taken responsibility for sin and suffering by sharing its results, including feeling abandoned in a hostile world. For Christians Jesus' resurrection is their proof.

21 Christian Beliefs: holiness

This unit explores what Christians believe about the character of God.

We start with a famous description of God from the Bible.

*In the year that King Uzziah died
I saw the Lord seated on a throne,
    high and exalted,
and the skirts of his robe filled the temple.
Seraphim were in attendance on him.
Each had six wings: with one pair of wings
they covered their faces,
and with another their bodies and with the
third pair they flew.
They were calling to one another,
'Holy, holy, holy is the Lord of Hosts: the
whole earth is full of his glory.'
As each called, the threshold shook to its
foundations at the sound
while the house began to fill with clouds of
smoke.
Then I said, 'Woe is me! I am doomed,
for my own eyes have seen the King, the Lord
of Hosts,
I, a man of unclean lips,
I, who dwell among a people of unclean lips.'
One of the seraphim flew to me, carrying in
his hand a glowing coal
which he had taken from the altar with a
pair of tongs.
He touched my mouth with it and said,
'This has touched your lips,
now your iniquity is removed and your sin is
wiped out.'* (Isaiah 6:1-7) **(1)**

The hymn of the angelic servants of God, called seraphim in this vision of the prophet Isaiah, has become part of the worship of many Christian churches.

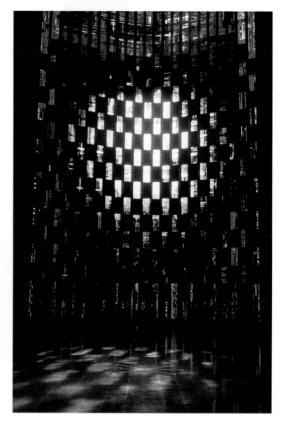

A John Piper's Baptistry window, Coventry Cathedral

Making it clear

List the things the word 'Holy' has been linked with so far in this book (for example, Holy Week).
Read extract (1). Is the link there mainly with:
- the temple
- God's character
- Isaiah's feelings?

Why do you think Christians call so many things 'Holy'?

Saints are specially honoured in the Orthodox Church because their lives show aspects of the character of God. Prayers are said before their icons.

B   A Greek Orthodox icon of a saint

'They're painted in a special way, you need special colours, otherwise they're not classed as an icon. The saints are always there where their icons are.'   (Stacey) **(2)**

Building bridges

In groups, decide what colours advertisers associate with:

● purity
● top quality.

Take examples from TV, magazines, hoardings, etc.

Now list the dominant colours in photos A and B. Do any of them match your findings from the advertisers?

What do you think the artists wanted to convey about the character of God? Read extract (2) for Stacey's ideas.

I believe in the Holy Spirit, the holy Catholic Church, the Communion of saints ...
          (Part of the Apostles' Creed) **(3)**

Although the word 'saint' in English is different from the word 'holy', the New Testament uses the same Greek word for both. In his first letter to Corinth, Paul tells the Christians there that they are 'called to be saints', that is 'holy'.
(1 Corinthians 1:2).   **(4)**

The love of God draws us to him, a redemptive love shown forth by Jesus Christ in his life and on the cross. As his disciples, we are called to live in the life and power of the Holy Spirit.
          (*Advices* of the Society of Friends) **(5)**

'For us God is a mystery we don't understand. We lost the unity with God when Adam and Eve decided they knew better. He came down himself as a man, then we rejected and crucified him. Now we believe we've got the Holy Spirit as our guide in our daily lives. That's what Christ promised us.

Our religion is our daily lives. We don't live our lives and reserve a little piece on a Sunday, or when we feel like it, to go to church. We go along living our religion, and loving I suppose. I mean, God is love and when you love everything else follows.'   (Stacey's mother) **(6)**

... the harvest of the Spirit is love, joy, peace, patience, kindness, goodness, fidelity, gentleness and self-control ...
          (Galatians 5:22–3) **(7)**

Working it out

Read extracts (3) and (4). In separate groups, brainstorm the words 'holy', 'church' and 'saints'.

Now read extracts (5)–(7). What do they add to your interpretation of each word? Share your findings. In what ways do Christians link 'holiness' with everyday life?

Thinking it through

Have you ever met or heard about anyone you would consider 'saintly'? Write a brief description of their character.

22 Christian beliefs: service

This unit concludes our exploration of some important Christian beliefs.

Our aim: to worship, to serve and to witness to Christ. (Christ Church, Coventry) **(1)**

Send us out, in the power of your Spirit, to live and work to your praise and glory.
(Closing prayer, Holy Communion service, Church of England) **(2)**

When you have a choice of employment, choose that which gives the fullest opportunity for the use of your talents in the service of your fellow-men.
(*Advices* of the Society of Friends) **(3)**

'Friends are concerned to work for the common good wherever they are. Doing the work there was to be done and quietly carrying on their worshipping life. If the people they were working with cared to join in, fine.

That's one thing that has led Friends to be able to work in places like the United Nations. We also have people who work in London, in the diplomatic community. They provide opportunities for people to meet who are unable, for political reasons, to be seen to meet.' (Alice's mother) **(4)**

'We've just started a new "mercy project", as we call it, helping to finance a mobile clinic for Azerbaijan. A qualified nurse is involved in the work. There are about a million refugees there so there's desperate need. We've been involved in similar projects with the Kurds and helping set up a home for orphaned children in Romania.'
(Abigail's father) **(5)**

'God uses us as channels of his power if we'll let ourselves be used. I believe that the Kingdom of God is where there are people who allow God to rule in their life. If people are obeying and listening to what he's saying then that's going to be good for society. A little beam of light can go through a lot of darkness.' (Abigail's mother) **(6)**

A Orphaned children and their new home, Romania (extract 5)

'With "Marches for Jesus" we join with other churches and we all go marching round the roads in a particular area. It's usually a planned route. There's a whole musical score written by Graham Kendrick, with songs and shouts, and we go through it time and again. Sometimes there are thousands of people. Quite often, at Easter or in September, we get lots of churches in Coventry involved.' (Abigail) **(7)**

Making it clear

Read extracts (1)–(3). The word 'service' seems to be used in several ways. Choose three out of the following which you think best explain its meaning:

- working in the church organization
- another word for an act of worship
- helping people outside the church
- something God has told you to do
- your ordinary job or career
- a special task in addition to your daily work.

Building bridges

In groups, each person should choose a type of 'service', e.g. bus, leisure, cleaning, etc. and write it on a card. (Use *Yellow Pages* or a local directory to help you, if you run out of ideas.) Now produce an argument in favour of your ideal of the 'service' you have chosen. Decide which 'service' has the most convincing arguments.

Which, if any, do you think a Christian might consider as a way of 'serving' God?

Working it out

In groups, collect items of current news, perhaps over a week, from local and national media. Choose one or two which give you particular cause for concern.

Decide what sort of action is going to be most effective in those situations, e.g. a demonstration, an international relief effort, a secret negotiation, an appeal.

Look at extracts (4), (5) and (7). Do any of them help you decide how your 'cause for concern' could be tackled?

Read extract (6). Now choose one of the other extracts referred to above. How might people in that situation think God is using them?

Thinking it through

Look at the last sentence of extract (6).

Write, in a few sentences what, in your experience, could count as 'light' shining in the 'darkness' *or* design a poster to illustrate this sentence.

B Medical aid for refugees in Africa

23 Growing up: expectations

This unit explores young people's ideas about careers and marriage.

What do you expect of life?

What do you think your life will be like when you're about 20?

'I hope I'll be at college or university. I don't know exactly what I'll be studying but I know I won't be well off. I think students are poor.'

Why go to college then?

'My parents want me to get good qualifications and have a good job. In an office, not a shop because my Dad thinks he works too hard. He doesn't have enough days off.' (Stacey) **(1)**

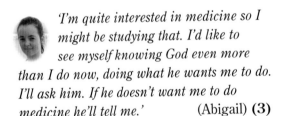
'I'd like to be a studenty type, wear all sorts of arty clothes because I love outrageous things.' (Alice) **(2)**

'I'm quite interested in medicine so I might be studying that. I'd like to see myself knowing God even more than I do now, doing what he wants me to do. I'll ask him. If he doesn't want me to do medicine he'll tell me.' (Abigail) **(3)**

Is there anything you wouldn't do?

'I wouldn't write horoscopes or tell fortunes. It's against my religion basically. God said not to look into the future. I couldn't do anything mixed with the occult for the same reason ... or anything dishonest.' (Andrew) **(4)**

'I couldn't make any armaments, things that kill people. So, if I was in engineering and I designed a machine to make things for industry, it could be difficult because people might be able to use it for making guns.' (Alice) **(5)**

Making it clear

Arrange the following in the order you think a Christian might put them when choosing a job.

- making money
- pleasing parents
- helping others
- avoiding harm
- serving God

What about marriage?

'I'm quite positive about it, but I don't think it's good to be married really young.' (Abigail) **(6)**

'I don't think marriage is absolutely necessary. You've got to live with someone before you marry them so you know what they're really like. I think marriage should be a solemnization of what you already feel, not something on top of everything else. So I might not get married.' (Alice) **(7)**

A Students at university

All Christian churches take marriage seriously. For some, including the Orthodox, it is a sacrament. For all it is a ceremony involving God as well as men and women.

The vows made by bride and groom vary slightly. Those traditional in the Church of England include the words: 'for better, for worse, for richer, for poorer, in sickness and in health, to love and to cherish till death us do part.'

At a Quaker wedding these words would be said after a period of silent prayer: 'Friends, I take this Friend (full name), to be my wife, promising with God's help, to be unto her a loving and faithful husband, so long as we both on earth shall live.'

The woman makes the same promises as her husband. The whole meeting then act as witnesses, believing God has heard the promises which have been made. **(10)**

B Signing the marriage certificate at a Quaker wedding

'I hope I'll get married to a Greek woman, probably before I'm thirty. My mother says she wants me to keep my religion as long as I can. If I marry an English woman then things like Easter, and when we're supposed to fast, will probably be forgotten.' (Stacey) **(8)**

'I don't know whether I will get married. But if I do I'll wait until I've got established in a good job.'

(Andrew) **(9)**

Working it out

Read extracts (6)–(10).

In groups, list some of the things which could have influenced each young person's attitude to marriage. Decide which could make them want to marry and which might make them hesitate. Share your results.

Thinking it through

Imagine you are involved in a discussion about marriage in which similar views to those of Abigail, Alice, Andrew and Stacey have been expressed. How would you reply to them with your own view?

Building bridges

In pairs, note the things which your parents think are most important in deciding your future. Which of them match those mentioned in extracts (1)–(9)?

24 Growing up: challenges

This unit introduces Christian responses to some moral issues.

What are you afraid of?

'Nothing, really.'
(Andrew and Abigail)

'Spiders!'
(Stacey, half joking?)

'I'm afraid of people not liking me.'
(Alice) **(1)**

What do you think about these things?

Smoking?

'It should be banned in public places because non-smokers like me can't avoid breathing in the fumes.'
(Stacey)

'It's a waste of money.' (Andrew)

'You're destroying a body which is very special.'
(Abigail) **(2)**

Alcohol?

'I don't smoke, but I don't think there's any harm if there's a group event and you bring drinks with alcohol and share them around. What I think is dangerous is if somebody gets hooked on it and takes a whole bottle to drink on their own.' (Alice)

'It's there for pleasure and Jesus obviously drank it, but I don't think it should be misused. When it's been drunk too much it's very bad. It wrecks people's lives.' (Abigail) **(3)**

Taking drugs?

'You could get addicted which could lead to more serious things.' (Andrew)

'Sometimes I suppose it isn't really their fault if they're going through something really bad. But I can't really see any reason for taking them at all.'
(Abigail)

'Anyone who takes drugs needs professional help.' (Stacey) **(4)**

Fighting wars?

'I respect the principles of people who refuse to fight. But if it was the last resort and you'd tried everything else, then in some cases it can't really be avoided.'
(Andrew)

When a nation defends itself against external aggression or when it rises up against an occupying power then that conflict, though tragic, is proper under the present conditions of human existence. (Church of England, *Peacemaking in a Nuclear Age*, 1988)

We utterly deny all outward wars and strife and fightings with outward weapons, for any end, or under any pretence whatever, this is our testimony to the whole world.
(Quaker *Peace Testimony*, 1660) **(5)**

A   United Nations 'peacekeeping' troops

Death?

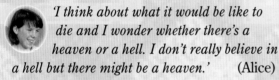

'I think about what it would be like to die and I wonder whether there's a heaven or a hell. I don't really believe in a hell but there might be a heaven.'   (Alice)

'I don't really want to go through any suffering or pain, but it'll be all right in the end provided I love God all my life. Hell is indescribable really, but I think of it as a place without God. Heaven means actually being able to see God and be with him.'
(Abigail) **(6)**

Love your enemies; do good to those who hate you; bless those who curse you; pray for those who treat you spitefully. Treat others as you would like them to treat you.
(Luke 6:27–8, 31) **(7)**

Do you not know that your body is a temple of the indwelling Holy Spirit, and the Spirit is God's gift to you? You do not belong to yourselves; you were bought at a price. Then glorify God in your body.
(1 Corinthians 6:19–20) **(8)**

Making it clear

List five things which it is sensible to be afraid of, and five which it would be foolish to be afraid of.

Compare your list with a partner. Do they include any referred to in this unit? Which of them can you influence by your own decisions?

Building bridges

Think of something which you might refuse to do because it was 'against your principles'. How would you explain the principle to a partner? Try to put it in one simple sentence.

Working it out

In groups, choose one of the issues in extracts (2)–(5). Read extracts (7) and (8). Decide which a Christian might turn to for guidance in approaching the issue. What evidence is there in the extract you chose that they have done so?

Thinking it through

Look at extract (1). It takes 'moral' courage to admit to weaknesses. Write your advice to Alice to help her resist 'peer group' pressure to do something against her principles so as not to appear different.

25 Commitment: possessions

This unit considers Christian attitudes to wealth.

'A tenth of my pocket money goes to charity, in theory! Sometimes I forget so I make it up next week. Usually I just put a pound in my "charity box" every so often.'

Who asked you to give a tenth?

'I just decided. Quite a lot of Christians give a tenth. Actually, my Mum and Dad did, so I thought I'd do it as well.'   (Andrew)

The 'tenth' Andrew's mother and father give supports several Christian activities. It includes charities which help people in need. Some of it pays for full-time ministers in the Church of England.   **(1)**

'I'm a member of a church committee called "Friends of the Poor". We are a registered charity and we get a lot of letters from people who want our help. We've given money to the cancer ward at the local hospital as well as helping with collections for the victims of earthquakes in different parts of the world.'   (Stacey's mother) **(2)**

Do you regard your possessions as given you in trust and do you part with them freely for the needs of others?

Do you give a right proportion of your money to support the work of the Society?

(*Queries* of the Society of Friends) **(3)**

As Christians all that we have, including our money, belongs to God. We are responsible to Him as stewards of His money, to use it for His glory. We need to consider carefully before God what we do with our money and act responsibly with all of it – not just that which we give away. A right attitude is essential for 'God loves a cheerful giver'.

(Coventry Christian Fellowship) **(4)**

Do not store up for yourselves treasure on earth, where moth and rust destroy, and thieves break in and steal; but store up treasure in heaven, where neither moth nor rust will destroy, nor thieves break in and steal. For where your treasure is there will your heart be also.

(Matthew 6:19–21) **(5)**

We believe in life before death

Do you?

Christian Aid Week May 16-21

with the support of The CO-OPERATIVE BANK

A   The charity Christian Aid uses the money donated to it to fund projects around the world to help people in need

Making it clear

Read extracts (1)–(4).

In pairs, arrange these statements in order, beginning with the ones you think most Christians would agree with:

- Personal possessions are worthless.
- Charity begins at home.
- Respond generously to appeals for help.
- Support your local church.
- Only give when you feel like it.
- Have a careful look at where your money is going.
- Treat possessions as a trust from God.

Add another of your own based on one of the extracts.

Building bridges

In a group decide on a 'cause' you feel strongly about. Form yourselves into a committee to raise money for it. Think of an appealing title. Design a poster to encourage people to commit themselves to regular donations. If possible think of a slogan to help people remember your cause.

Working it out

Read extract (5). It is one of Jesus' many sayings on the subject of possessions.

In groups, take on the role of a church committee. Your task is to decide how to use a legacy of £10,000. For example you could:

- beautify the church
- pay more full-time workers
- support a local charity
- invest the money in case of an emergency
- respond to an international appeal
- support another struggling church
  – or, of course, do something quite different.

Explain how your decision has been influenced by Jesus' teaching, in extract (5).

Thinking it through

Look at extract (1). The idea of 'tithing' is to set apart a proportion of your possessions, in this case a tenth, regularly, for example every week. Christians who do this believe that it shows God that they take their Christian beliefs (commitment) seriously. It also helps them remember that all their possessions were given them by God to be used in the way he wants (extracts (3) and (4)).

Think of something you have done for the sake of a cause or an ideal (e.g. giving time, money, work, 'dedicating' something).

Explain to a partner how you felt when you were actually doing the 'dedicating'.

B Money offered as part of worship

26 Commitment: food and drink

This unit looks at the way Christians, particularly the Orthodox, use fasting to show their personal commitment to God.

'We're not allowed to eat meat on Wednesdays and Fridays.'

All through the year?
'Yes, because Christ died on a Friday, I'm not sure about Wednesdays.'

A Fish and chips – a family business

Are there any other things you don't eat at particular times?
'Yes, when we fast 40 days before Christmas and 50 days before Easter. I don't actually go straight into the fasting. First of all I don't eat meat and then two weeks before Easter I don't eat eggs or any sort of dairy product or oil or animal fats.'

You wouldn't eat cakes?
'No, just things like olives, bread. We have tea but without milk.'

Would other members of your family be fasting more than you?
'My mum fasts right through.'

(Stacey) **(1)**

'If you can have no oil at all throughout fasting then it's all the better for you, but the weather here doesn't help. You need something inside you to stop you getting ill, so you have to eat.' (Stacey's mother) **(2)**

Stacey's family are cooking in oil for an occupation, can't they eat the food themselves?
'Actually that was a point we brought up when we were talking to the priest. We said, "We're always tempted by the food, it's very difficult for us not to eat. You're smelling chickens and you're thinking, 'Isn't that lovely!' When you're tempted by it are you committing a sin?".' (Stacey's mother) **(3)**

'He said, "God accepts your fasting better because you're in cooking all the time. You're looking at it and yet you're saying to yourself, 'No, I'm not going to have that.' So, if you're living with temptation it means you've got a stronger will and your faith is stronger than the monks or the nuns who actually only cook what they can eat (i.e. what their rules allow them to eat). It's a living. You can't stop living because you're fasting."'
(Stacey's mother) **(4)**

B An Orthodox monk collects medicinal plants, Mount Athos, Greece. The regular practice of fasting is part of the way of life in an Orthodox monastic community

> *When you fast do not look gloomy like the hypocrites: they make their faces unsightly so that everyone can see that they are fasting. Truly I tell you they have their reward already. But when you fast anoint your head and wash your face, so that no one sees that you are fasting, but only your Father who is in secret; and your father who sees what is done in secret will give you your reward.*
>
> *(Matthew 6:16–18)* **(5)**

Making it clear

Read extracts (1)–(4).
Which of the following statements best describes Orthodox views on fasting?

- Everybody has to do it.
- It only applies to monks and nuns.
- You have a choice, it's up to you.
- You can't eat anything forbidden.
- You can use your common sense.

Building bridges

In groups, form yourselves into a 'secret society'. Decide on something which each member should do regularly to prove their loyalty. (Make it practical, not harmful or impossible.)

Don't tell anybody. Write it down on a blank card. Exchange cards with another group. Decide whether their 'proof of loyalty' is:

- easy
- fairly hard
- very hard.
  Share your results.

Working it out

Write the heading 'The purpose of fasting is to help you'.

In pairs, give four answers, one for each person represented in the extracts (i.e. Stacey, Stacey's mother, the priest, Jesus) adding others if you can. For example, the Wednesday fast, which Stacey mentioned, is a reminder of Jesus' betrayal by Judas, so one answer could be: 'To help Christians remember Jesus' sufferings by depriving themselves.'

Compare your results.

Thinking it through

Either Explain what advantages fasting might have over other ways of showing a personal commitment to God (e.g. giving money to charity).

Or Note down any ways in which you discipline yourself, or prove to yourself that something or someone is more important than you (e.g. a 'famine lunch' for Oxfam).

27 Commitment: responsibilities

This unit looks at how the Society of Friends gives responsibilities to young people.

'JYF Weekends (the initials stand for Junior Young Friends) are held three times a year, usually in Quaker meeting houses around Birmingham. I'm on the organizing committee so we have two meetings beforehand to arrange things.

On the weekend we arrive on the Friday night, we eat our tea and talk to everybody. We have a system so everybody can go to bed when they want.

"Early beds" is from about 10 to 10.30pm. Those who just want to talk quietly, then go to sleep, go into one room and no one disturbs them. Everybody else just stays around until they want to go to sleep. Most people usually talk until about half past three! We catch up on what's happened to everybody over half a year or so.

On Saturday morning we all get up, have breakfast, then usually we have a speaker on a particular issue – vegetarianism, Amnesty, freedom, for example.

Then we have drinks and discussions. It's free time in the afternoon so we can go bowling or ice-skating or swimming.

Every night, Friday and Saturday, we have "epilogue" about 10pm. We all sit round in a circle. Usually there are candles in the middle and we switch off the lights. Sometimes we hold hands and sit for quarter of an hour or twenty minutes in silence. On Saturday night we all usually go to bed straight afterwards because we're a bit tired.

Sunday morning we get up and cook the breakfast. We clear up and then, usually, have a business meeting. People are organized to write to the clerk of the meeting and people who've provided food and other adults who've been helping.

Then we all go into the Meeting for Worship.'

(Alice) **(1)**

A   A Junior Young Friends committee meeting

We aim to provide a weekend which is happy, exploratory, Quaker-based and, to the largest extent possible, run by us. We try to bring young Quakers together, and we hope that people's views are challenged and inspired by the themes, that the weekend has a supportive, friendly atmosphere, but above all that they are FUN!

Who can come?
Generally JYFs are young Quakers aged from eleven to about sixteen, from the Warwickshire Monthly Meeting area. We are glad to serve as an outreach to young people in general so current JYFs may bring friends.

(JYF Charter) **(2)**

The JYF Charter spells out the organization and rules which have been agreed. They include:

- the roles of 'Responsible Adults' (one adult of each sex, usually one of 'parental age' and one from the meeting hosting the weekend)
- sleeping (sleeping bags on the floor), catering, cleaning and medical arrangements
- committee membership ('six or seven young people, mostly from the older end with two representatives of the younger end')
- rules, which begin, 'Everyone attending has responsibility for themselves and to the group as a whole'. **(3)**

Making it clear
Make a list of the things Alice will have to help organize. Check your list with a partner.

Working it out
In groups, form yourselves into a committee to decide the rest of the 'rules' for a residential youth weekend. Refer to all three extracts for the sort of things you need to consider. What other issues might arise? Compare your results.

Thinking it through
Have you ever had to be responsible for a lot of other people? How did you feel?
    Did it all turn out well or did anything go wrong? Tell your experience to a partner and compare it with theirs.

B   A panel from a Quaker tapestry

28 Belonging: our country

This unit begins to explore the idea of identity and its links with religion.

'Who am I?' and 'Where do I belong?'

The young people interviewed for this book are all British, but you can be British in a variety of ways. They were asked which of a number of words described them. They could add others which weren't on the list. It began with 'European'.

Andrew said,

'European, British and English because I live in Britain and I was born there and my parents are British.'

Are you happy being European and British?
'Yes!'

Abigail said,

'European, British, half Welsh and, yes, English. Part of it is where you're born and where your parents come from but I feel part of the community.'

Stacey began, not with European, but with British, then added some others.

What makes you feel you're British and Middle Eastern and Greek Cypriot, all those things together?

'Well, firstly because I was born in Britain, but my family originated in Cyprus and you've got to distinguish the Greek Cypriots from the Turkish Cypriots.'

Alice was a bit unhappy with some of these labels.

'European? Yes. British sounds a bit like "enclosed and narrow-minded". I'd like to be Welsh, I like Wales. Scotland's a nice place but I'm not Scottish. English is more narrow-minded than British, but I suppose I am English. I'd like to be Irish as well!'

What makes you feel like this?
'Well people are people the world over, no matter who they are.'

A 'Our country': town

B 'Our country': countryside

Building bridges

Here is the list used in the interviews.
Do a class survey based on it.
Which of these do you identify with?

- European
- British
- African
- Welsh
- West Indian
- Asian
- Scottish
- Eastern European
- English
- Irish
- Indian
- any other

Working it out

Abigail felt she was part of the local community although she was half Welsh. Stacey felt part of several 'communities'.

Using this and any other evidence you can think of, in pairs, note down some of the other things which are important in giving people a sense of identity.

Add to your class survey on the basis of these findings.

Thinking it through

Read Alice's response to the questions.

Why do you think Alice is uncertain whether she wants to be 'British'? In groups, note down three reasons you could give to help her change her mind.

29 Belonging: our Church

This unit explores the way religions help to give people a sense of identity.

The young people were asked what name they would give to their religion.

Three of them said 'Christianity' but each, then, went on to try to describe the Christian denomination to which they belong.

Andrew said,

'I go to a Church of England but I'm not strongly "Church of England".'

Do your parents belong to the Church of England?

'Yes, but we go to Baptists and anywhere that's suitable.'

What does being suitable mean?

'Which worships in the best way, does things in the best way and has the best vicar.'

Stacey said,

'Christian Orthodox.'

Are they the same?

'Well, Christian is "believing in Christ" and Orthodox is "hasn't been changed over the years". It's closer to the truth than just ordinary Christians. That's what I've been taught.'

Would you just call yourself Orthodox or Greek Orthodox?

'Greek Orthodox.'

What do you think is special about being Orthodox?

'Just being different from everybody else!'

Abigail said,

'Christianity, probably "Free Church" because we're not strictly Church of England or Baptist or anything, that's how we describe it anyway.'

What's special about that?

'We haven't got rules and regulations because we feel that people should know what's right and that God should tell them.'

Alice said,

'I think of myself as a Quaker first, I'm not very sure whether I'm a Christian or not.'

What's special about being a Quaker?

'There are no dogmas or creeds, no one to tell you what to believe. You find out for yourself what you believe. It's a bit difficult to be a Christian if you don't really know what being a Christian means. I think that it's generally believing in Christ. I think that maybe I believe in Christ in the way that he was a very good person. He loved people and that was a really good way to live.'

Each denomination has its own statements of what it believes and practices. Some of these, such as the Church of England's 'Articles of Religion' and the decisions of the Ecumenical Councils accepted by the Orthodox Church, are too detailed to include here.

We are a Church of orthodox belief – upholding the ancient creeds of the Church, and seeking to express a biblical faith in our church life together.
We are committed to the mission of the Church – both at home and abroad – as the natural outworking of Christ's command ... to 'make disciples of all nations'.

(Part of the statement of belief from the Coventry Christian Fellowship)

A 'Christ in Glory', a tapestry by Graham Sutherland in Coventry Cathedral

Study the Bible intelligently, using the help available from modern sources. Make every effort to understand the Christian faith. Be ready at all times to receive fresh light from whatever quarter it may come; approach new theories with discernment. Remember our testimony that Christianity is not a notion but a way. (*Advices* of the Society of Friends)

Making it clear

Which young person thought the following was most important in the denomination to which they belonged?

- being free to find out for yourself
- being closely linked to the past
- having the right style of worship
- being responsive to the guidance of God

Building bridges

In pairs, note down three or four things that make you feel you belong to 'your' school (or your form).

Now look at the school's 'Aims'. Which, if any, match your reasons for 'belonging'?

What would you tell a new student who had joined your class was most important about belonging to your school?

Working it out

In pairs, compare Abigail's and Alice's answers, noting down any similarities.

Now do the same with the statements from their denominations.

Are there any differences between what the young people emphasize and what their denominations emphasize?

Note down what you think makes them feel that they 'belong', whether or not they accept all that their denomination says is important.

Thinking it through

Note down your own answers to the questions: 'Who am I?' and 'Where do I belong?' Use the headings: 'Things I'm sure about' and 'Still making up my mind'.

Now look at the answers of one of the young people to the questions about country and religion. How do their certainties and hesitations compare with yours?

30 Belonging: our experience

This unit explores the experience of being a young Christian in Britain today.

The young people featured in this book were all born into Christian families. All of them felt their parents encouraged them and supported them in their faith. But they all said that being a Christian was really up to them.

For Andrew,

Christianity is unique in the fact that you choose to be a Christian, you aren't born into it. If your parents are Christian it doesn't make you a Christian. Their parents can try and make a person a Christian. But they won't be able to be a Christian just because their parents say so. It's inside yourself, it's not physical.'

Alice said,

'I don't just accept what my parents say. I think about it first and compare it to what other people think. Religion's got to be something you don't just do on a Sunday. Not like just going to a church and someone tells you what you're meant to be doing. It's got to be really you.'

Having a religious commitment didn't necessarily make life easy. Stacey, in particular, felt that being Orthodox meant

'being different from everybody else, I suppose.'

At school he only talked seriously about his religion to a Buddhist friend.

Being the odd one out was also Abigail's experience. Especially in her first year at secondary school, she was called names and treated badly by other pupils.

'Just because I didn't swear and didn't keep stirring things people said, "Stop trying to be so good," and that sort of thing.'

How did you react?

'You can ignore it or you can say something snide back, but I thought, maybe I've got other things that make up for it. I think it's just patience. I think God's helped me through that. I don't know what he's done but it's something, so now they respect me more.'

Is religion important to you?

'Yes, very. I'd be a totally different person without it. I'd miss the love and security and being able to talk to God whenever I feel like it.'

Is there anything else you want to say about being a Christian?

'Only that really I think it's the only way, because what's going to happen to you when you die?'

Some people would say that was a very selfish way of looking at things.

'I can see their point of view. But only someone who wasn't a Christian would say that because they wouldn't know what it's like from the inside. It's all very well saying, "You're being very selfish," but what happens when you die is just a very small part of being a Christian. You're not being selfish because that's where God wants you to be.'

Making it clear

According to these young people, being a Christian involves:

- being born into it
- being taught it by your parents
- deciding for yourself
- being just like everybody else
- being prepared to be different
- knowing God personally.

Decide which of these statements fit the evidence.

Building bridges

If you were asked to choose something which was important to you as a person what would it be? Explain your choice to a partner.

Now look at what Abigail, Alice, Andrew and Stacey chose. Which of their 'important things' is most like yours?

Working it out

In groups, using this unit and any other evidence you have, list some ways in which taking a religion seriously can make you the 'odd one out'. Compare your results.

Now, against as many items as possible on your list, note how you think their religion supports people in these situations.

Thinking it through

Look back through this book and make your own private checklist of any similar things in your life that help you face difficult questions and decisions (e.g. people, groups, activities, beliefs, experiences).

A   Abigail: a song based on a text from the New Testament

Each young person chose something important to them:

Stacey: the icon that hangs by his bed

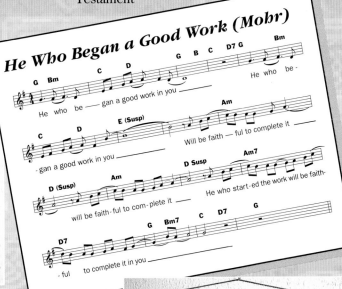

C   Alice: an extract from a Quaker anthology

All my life I've heard, 'God is love', without understanding what was meant. Recently I've come to feel that in a very real way G-d/ess IS the love that flows in and between and among us. The ebb and flow of my commitment to love, to peace, to harmony makes G-d/ess stronger or weaker in my heart.

Rose Ketterer, 1987

D   Andrew: a poster from his bedroom

63

Index

The numbers in **bold** tell you where to find the most detailed information.